the PAGAN mysteries of Halloween

the PAGAN
mysteries
of
Halloween

Celebrating the Dark Half of the Year

By Jean Markale

Translated by Jon Graham

INNER TRADITIONS
Rochester, VT

Inner Traditions International
One Park Street
Rochester, Vermont 05767
www.InnerTraditions.com

First U.S. edition published by Inner Traditions in 2001

Originally published in French under the title Halloween: histoire et traditions by
Éditions Imago

Library of Congress Cataloging-in-Publication Data

Markale, Jean.
    [Halloween : histoire et traditions. English]
    The pagan mysteries of Halloween : celebrating the dark half of the year / by Jean Markale ; translated by Jon Graham.
        p. cm.
    ISBN 0-89281-900-6 (pbk.)
    1. Halloween. I. Title.
    GT4965 .M256 2001
    394.2646—dc21

2001003400

Printed and bound in Canada

10 9 8 7 6 5 4 3 2 1

Text design and layout by Cindy Sutherland
This book was typeset in Baskerville MT

Inner Traditions wishes to express its appreciation for assistance given by the government of France through the Ministère de la Culture in the preparation of this translation.

Nous tenons à exprimer nos plus vifs remerciements au government de la France et le ministère de la Culture pour leur aide dans le préparation de cette traduction.

contents

Introduction

It is an autumn evening, the evening of October 31, to be precise. A biting wind churns the clouds and tears the last leaves from the trees to send them spinning every which way over the damp ground, rich with the fragrances of autumn. It is the end of the day, the beginning of the night, that twilight period when light and shadow commingle and it is difficult to determine where one ends and the other starts. In appearance it is a simple autumn evening, like any other. However, in the villages and cities as well as in the remote rural regions lost in the valleys, there is something else going on, something out of the ordinary.

It can be seen first in the behavior of the men and women leaving work. They appear relaxed, if not happy. They linger willingly in the bars, or, if they have returned straight home, they have done so knowing that tomorrow they will have broken the infernal cycle of work for a day. Ah! It is true. The next day is a holiday, what was formerly called, under the *Ancien Régime*, a "church solemnity," or a religious festival, which even the very secular French Republic has preserved in the official calendar, to the satisfaction of all its citizens, both believers and nonbelievers.

It is, in fact, All Saints' Day. However, in the minds of most people it is a sad day. Families make visits to the cemetery to leave chrysanthemums on the tombs of the dearly departed. This ritual gesture of commemoration of the deceased is usually accompanied by a kind of sorrow that the weather often echoes. When it is raining or the sky is "low and heavy," as Baudelaire pounded out in evocation of the hammer blows necessary to build a scaffold, don't most people say it is All Saints' Day weather, even if it occurs in the middle of spring?

Once the night has grown darker, bizarre apparitions make their appearance. Someone knocks at the door. You open it and find yourself in the presence of a strange mob of boys and girls. Their faces are blackened, or they wear large white sheets or some-times even grimacing masks and witches' hats on their heads, and they all scream lugubrious "Boos!" for the sake of the person open-ing the door. And these children are clamoring for cakes, candy, apples, or even a couple of coins. It is in your best interest to give them something, for if you do not, they are capable of casting a curse upon your home and, especially, of returning later in the night to haunt it, disturbing the sleep of the inhabitants or giving them abominable nightmares. What's this all about?

This is when you spot on your neighbors' windowsill—if you have any neighbors!—an enormous pumpkin that has been visibly hollowed out and had holes carved in its shell depicting eyes and a mouth. Inside, the flame of a candle is dancing to the will of the wind. This depiction brings to mind a grimacing death's-head, and that produces a gripping effect, all the more so when you realize that all the neighbors—if you have neighbors—have been given the same order and have acted in the same fashion. Truly, one can-not be faulted for asking just what it all means.

It is not Carnival, nor even Christmas. In fact, one refrains from displaying such grotesque figures at Christmas. The recuper-ation of the profoundly Christian festival of All Saints' Day by a populace that does not have too clear an idea of just what the day corresponds to, though grasps that it concerns a sacred commem-oration excluding any morbid or diabolical reference, results in the main focus centering on celebrating and feasting. So you may have some questions, but all at once, you recall that for at least the past two weeks stores have been sporting some strange and fantastic decorations in their windows. It makes for a great rivalry, if not in bad taste, at least in exaggeration. Here are seen dolls depicting passably terrifying devils, witches either on their broomsticks or casting magic spells, monsters of all kinds emerging from the most delirious recesses of the imagination, not to mention the fake skeletons, which are excellent imitations of the real thing. At bakeries you can even find excellent cakes in horrible shapes: almond paste dragons, spice bread gnomes, animals emerging straight out of *Jurassic Park* dripping with food coloring, and cream puffs that bring to mind phantoms in their winding sheets more than the honorable vegetable from which little boys are supposedly born.* All this is complemented by the numerous posters inviting the populace to various balls or demonstrations that "smell of brimstone." And of course all the produce merchants have displays offering a huge assortment of pumpkins, some of which have been carved like those that adorn your neighbors' windows.

True, this is the privileged season before the chill of winter arrives when these cucurbits of a sometimes impressive volume are cooked, permitting mothers to offer their children those good-for-you "squash soups" that the young ones accept while making faces behind their mothers' backs.

By all evidence, a curious ambience reigns over all of the Western world on October 31, and this ambience, almost completely absent in Europe for almost the entirety of the twentieth century, has enjoyed growing popularity there over the past dozen years, to the extent that its manifestations are becoming an institution comparable to those of Christmas, New Year's Day, and, to a lesser extent, because these festivals have weakened considerably, Mardi Gras and Mid-Lent. What we are talking about, of course, is Halloween.

The term evokes nothing for French speakers, who have adopted it nevertheless. It is much more familiar to Anglo-Saxons, on the one hand because it is an Old English word, and on the other hand

---

* The French term for cream puff is *choux à la crème,* literally "cabbage with cream," though *cabbage* in this instance refers not to the vegetable but to the flaky pastry that is multilayered like a cabbage. And just as storks supposedly bring children in some cultures, in France little boys are born in cabbage patches. —*Trans.*

because this apparent folk festival has never ceased being celebrated in the British Isles and in the United States. The defining feature of folk festivals is to provoke enthusiasm within all classes of a determined society. Such is the case for the mysterious Halloween.

We need first to reflect upon the date: the night preceding the first day of November. This date is no chance selection. And the night following the first day of November, the eve of November 2, corresponds, in the liturgical calendar of the Roman Catholic Church, to the Day of the Dead. That, too, is no accident.

Furthermore, in the general sense, All Saints' Day—which is by its very nature a festival of joy—is always confused with the Day of the Dead. This explains and justifies the placing of flowers on tombs, a ritual gesture that is both the manifestation of the memory of those who are no longer and a respectful homage in their honor. What we have here is a kind of "ancestor worship" that dares not say its name.

The Roman Catholic Church, like the various Protestant churches, has always encouraged, while energetically refusing any reference to ancestor worship, the acts of piety accompanying the first and second days of November. Toussaint (All Saints' Day), being literally the holiday of *all the saints,* whether officially recognized or not, could not be otherwise, inasmuch as Christian dogma assumes that any deceased individual, based on his merits, can be admitted among the Elect. But where the Roman church cannot venture any further is in the profane domain of the carnival-like manifestations of Halloween. This is why, on the eve of All Saints' Day in 1999, French bishops published a text severely condemning these manifestations in the name of dignity and respect owed the deceased and the Communion of Saints.

From a logical point of view, this condemnation is perfectly defendable because it denounces the inevitable abuses and excesses that accompany these kinds of manifestations. But from a liturgical point of view, it rings false with respect to the archetypes that have provoked these carnival-like manifestations, on the one hand, and on the other, their appropriate religious recuperation under an abbreviated form by the Church itself, which would have been unable to do otherwise. This is, in fact, to claim that the profane rituals of Halloween are the degenerated remainders of religious ceremonies celebrated within the sanctuary. In reality, as we will see later, it is these oft-decried profane rituals that are at the origin of Christian ceremonies.

Furthermore, it seems that this condemnation on the part of the French bishops is rather late in coming. In the past, the Church has not refrained from intervening in numerous circumstances of public life, even in cases where it was unwarranted. This was the case for "Father Christmas," who was deemed pagan and yet was a widespread presence in Christian families. It is true that the Roman Catholic Church joined here with the Protestant churches, mainly the Calvinists, for whom all festivals, including celebrations, arc not only useless but also pernicious, because they divert the individual from what should be his sole concern: ensuring his salvation. The festival forms part of those "deceptive powers" that, according to French philosopher Blaise Pascal, raise a smokescreen between daily life and its supreme objective. Finding themselves incapable of eradicating festivals of any kind, Christianity bent its combined efforts to endeavor to channel and give them a finality in accord with its fundamental dogmas.

But in the case of Halloween, it is the abrupt resurgence of profane festivities and their growing success in the past decade in France that provoked this reaction from the bishops, whose name, we should recall, signifies in the etymological sense no more nor less than "supervisors" (from the Greek *epi-skopein,* "observers above").

This brings up the question: From where came this sudden craze for such folkloric displays that are simultaneously macabre and impertinent and that carry the mark of an entire series of fantasies out of collective memory? Generally the answer is that it came from America. Certainly, since the beginning of this century, in fact from the time of the First World War, which the Europeans were able to bring to an end thanks to the intervention of the United States, what has been dubbed the "American model" has been gradually imposed throughout Europe—and indeed the entire world—and has been considerably reinforced since the Second World War. The influence of this American model has been felt on every level, from the best (in science and technology, mainly) to the worst ("skyscrapers"—those infernal towers—intensive agriculture, the improper use of chemical products, and so on), and, most especially in fashion, that absurdity worthy of Panurge's* sheep.

The contemporary European model of Halloween certainly comes from an imitation of what has been happening for a long time in the United States. But luckily, those dirtied and disguised children on the evening of October 31 can respond to the question of where Halloween comes from in a very clear and exact manner: Ireland. And this is the absolute truth, or at least a part of the truth. For while it is true that the carnival-like displays of Halloween in France and the rest of the European continent have been inspired by the American model, they are still nonetheless originally from western Europe, and the British Isles, in particular, where they have never ceased being observed.

On reflection, this appears quite normal: Americans are for the most part descendants of European emigrants gone in search of their fortunes on the other side of the Atlantic. If we subtract the autochthonous Amerindian component (a fairly reduced presence by the very fault of these conquering emigrants who were both colonists and willing slaughterers), the American tradition is a melting pot that sometimes cooks up a confused blend of various European traditions, in which the Anglo-Saxon and Celtic cultures are predominant. New York is incontestably the largest Irish city in the world, which lends weight to the assumption of the importance of the Irish contribution to the American mentality, and conse-

---

* Panurge, whose name means "all action," is a character, symbolic of the less likable traits in every man, in Rabelais's work *Gargantua and Pantagruel*. Although a cheat, a liar, and a coward, he offers enough redemptive features to encourage Pantagruel to keep him as a companion. "Panurge's sheep" refers to an incident in the fourth book in which he buys a sheep from a long-winded and pompous livestock dealer. Once the deal is concluded he hurls the animal into the sea, whereupon the rest of the flock follow suit, carrying with them the sheep dealer, who could not restrain them.—*Trans.*

quently the influence Ireland was able to exercise over certain specific folk customs that have presently fallen into what is known as the public domain.

But when contributions from the outside are integrated into a new culture, they are never gratuitous additions. By all evidence they correspond to a fundamental need on the part of those who welcome and incorporate them into their own culture. Every popular phenomenon, custom, belief, and ritual belongs to a collective memory, or in other words to fundamental myths that are devoid of meaning in and of themselves. Only a materialization—that is, a veritable "incarnation" within a specific social setting, with terms that are appropriate—can give them life and consequently make them intelligible.

Such is the case with Halloween. First, it is not an isolated phenomenon, as it has spread to many countries on the planet, although those who practice the ritual of this masquerade-festival do not have a very good idea of what it really means. Halloween has been orally passed down from generation to generation. It is thereby a tradition in the strict sense of the word, which is to say, "something that is transmitted," even if the why and how of what is being transmitted have been forgotten.

Rituals, oral tales, common sayings—these are perhaps the sole authentic testimonies to a universal tradition that was one at its origin but has fragmented over the course of the millennia. Its profound meaning is often lost, and all that remains is the skeletal framework around which a narrative, if not a veritable liturgy, may develop. These resemble what Jung calls archetypes, but which would more likely be errant mythological themes that have lost all logical connection to the central nucleus.

Because logic, to use this word in the sense that it has been understood since Aristotle, is absent from such a debate. All that matters is the relationship of the event, in this instance the ritual of Halloween, with what prompted it. One may attempt to define this relationship through the history of modes of thought, taking into account certain directions due to information gleaned here and there in what is properly considered history.

With regard to the essence of Halloween, all directions—which can multiply, stray, and find themselves at an impasse—nevertheless depart from the same central point: somewhere in the insular Celtic countries. That is where we must go in search of its origin.

So, if we truly wish to grasp the meaning of this carnival-like festival called Halloween and the profound reasons behind its association with All Saints' Day—of which it is but one aspect, in reality—it is necessary to travel back through the centuries, in search of time lost in some way, or rather time forgotten, by exploring the shadowy zones that have sheltered not only their development but also their justification. One thing is certain: surprises will not be lacking.

one

✝

the celtic festival
of samhain

Is Halloween a profane or a religious festival? Today this question is raised in the context of a secular society that holds that daily life, and consequently civic and public life, and spiritual life, or in other words adherence to this religion or that trend of thought, have no points in common; the citizen is free to think what he likes. This principle is one of tolerance, but a poorly understood tolerance. In all ancient societies, spiritual life was in no way separate from material life. There was no distinction between *sacred* and *profane,* and so we are forced to acknowledge that Halloween is a festival that is both sacred and profane.

In fact, the word *Halloween,* incontestably of Anglo-Saxon origin, comes from the undoubtedly popular contraction of All-(Saints')-Eve, which literally means the "eve of all the saints," with a shift in meaning: "holy evening" or "sacred evening." The reference could not be any more Christian . . . nor any more explicit.

Now Christianity, as is well known, grafted itself onto older religions that had their own customs and beliefs. The long struggle waged by the church fathers against the surviving aspects of paganism, then the pontifical or synodic injunctions against practices considered to be diabolical, clearly reveal that the Christian religion has never been able to eliminate certain concepts inherited from the dawn of time. Being unable to eliminate them, the Christian Church absorbed them by giving them what could be called in some respects their baptism certificate. This is how the period of Christmas, which corresponds to the winter solstice, exactly re-creates the reversal of values that took place in Roman society during the time of Saturnalia. This was the time when the king became subject, the subject became king, the master became slave, and the slave became master. Is this so different from the fact that Jesus, God incarnate, was born in the most total destitution inside a miserable grotto filled with the coldest drafts of winter air? Furthermore, doesn't this grotto—quickly transformed into a stable—bring to mind the myth of the Eastern god Mithra, the Sol Invictus, who was miraculously born from the sides of a virgin grotto, an event that took place on the evening of December 24? When establishing their liturgical calendar, the Christians drew from wherever they could, which is to say from the calendars of the so-called pagan societies that preceded the Christian era.

The same holds for the fixation of November 1 as the date for commemoration of all the saints "past, present, and to come." Because, despite the subtleties it is necessary to keep in mind when supplying an overly precise dating—and thus one that corresponds too strictly to one reality—we have to concede that the Christian festival of All Saints' Day and the carnival-like displays of Halloween are located precisely in the very time the Celts celebrated the great festival of Samhain during the era of the druids.

✢ The Festival of Samhain in the Celtic Calendar

Since the time of the High Middle Ages, the rhythm of life in western Europe has been based on the so-called "Gregorian" calendar (introduced by Pope Gregory the Great), which is nothing but a simple reformed version of the "Julian" calendar, which was apparently inspired by Julius Caesar. The Gregorian is a solar calendar, based on a year of 365 1/4 days, with a leap year every four years, and strictly follows the ellipsoidal course of the earth around the sun. This allows for the annual repetition of certain festivals on fixed days, such as Christmas, or, more prosaically, the celebration of the 1918 Armistice on November 11, Veterans Day, or the taking of the Bastille on July 14.

This undeniably practical aspect should not mask a completely different calendrical reality. Since remotest antiquity, not to mention prehistory, there have been—and still are—different ways of reckoning and organizing the days of the year. It could be thought surprising that the great Christian festival of Easter is never on the same date from year to year (and that the exact date of this festival was calculated differently by orthodox Christians). This is because the Christian Church, since its inception, sought to graft its liturgical cycle onto Hebrew points of reference: the Passion of Jesus Christ and his resurrection are closely linked to the Jewish Passover. Now, the Jews had not a solar calendar but a calendar of the lunar type, built on the immutable twenty-eight-day lunar cycle, meaning the actual duration of the moon's complete course around the earth.

Calendrical differences provide a fairly plausible explanation for the quarrels that broke out between the insular Celtic Christians and the dwellers on the Continent enfeoffed to the Roman church regarding the dating of the Easter holiday.[1] The calendar of the Celtic people was also of the lunar type. We know this, on the one hand, thanks to a broken Gallic bronze calendar that was discovered as a display of 149 fragments in Coligny (Ain) and is now housed in the archaeological museum of Lyon. On the other hand, this information is available to us thanks to countless Irish texts in the Gaelic language, transcribed by Christian monks but unquestionably of a traditional oral origin. Based on these it has been thought that the Celtic year was divided into twelve lunar months of twenty-eight days, with a thirteenth intercalary month intended to make the lunar and solar cycles coincide. Of course, this assumes that all the Celtic festivals, which depend on the lunar cycle, could never be celebrated on the same date, as is the case for the Christian holiday of Easter, which necessarily entails a movable dating method for Ascension and Pentecost, two holidays inti-mately linked to that of the resurrection of Christ. It is therefore clear that the problem of accurate dating posed by the Celtic festi-val calendar is far from simple, and that it is necessary to put Halloween—that is to say, the great druidic festival of Samhain—back into its original context.

The Christian calendar aims at universality and a kind of eter-nal return, but the Celtic calendar concerns itself more with the interactions between living beings and the cosmos, considered to be an indivisible totality. It is this close rapport between the indi-vidual and the cosmos that conditions the flow of time through the entire year for the Celts. In contrast to how time flows for the Romans, the stages of this period are not fixed in a regular, even static, thus purely symbolic fashion. They are flexible, wed to a cos-mic rhythm that could be compared to a slow respiration consist-ing of an irregular succession of inhalations and exhalations.

One would think that in order to be in harmony with this cos-mic breath, it is enough to scrupulously observe the most conspicu-ous points of the solar year—to wit, the solstices and the equinoxes. It so happens that this is not at all the case with the Celts: no Celtic festival is celebrated on the solstice or the equinox.* The four essential dates punctuating the Celtic year present a shift of forty to fifty days with respect to the solstice or equinox. This is a fact, and it is impossible to know the precise reason for it. Taking into account the explicit testimony of Caesar—corroborated by other Greek and Roman authors—according to which the druids "debate much on the stars and their movements, on the magnitude of the world and the earth,"[2] it is not out of astronomical igno-rance that these great festivals were shifted this way. The druids knew perfectly well what they were doing, and even though it is

---

*This is contrary to the claims of contemporary neo-druids and other Celtomaniacs who stubbornly persist in celebrating the most fanciful rituals on the occasion of the solstices, the summer solstice in particular. The solstice-based fes-tivals are much more ancient, dating back to prehistoric times; the information we have allows us to assume they were celebrated greatly during the Bronze Age. The famous "fires of Saint John" are the very remote extensions of these festivals.

impossible to know the profound reasons for their actions, one may, however, assume that their calendrical calculations were established based on the lunar cycle.

This omnipresent lunar cycle provokes quite a number of other unique features. According to Caesar's testimony, the Gauls considered the fall of night to be the beginning of the official day,* a custom also found among the Jews, who also followed a lunar calendar. Furthermore, in Celtic custom the twenty-eight-day month began on the night of the full moon. Consequently, dating the principal holidays of the Celtic year at November 1, February 1, May 1, and August 1 is solely a matter of convenience. In reality the holiday in question was necessarily placed on the night of the closest full moon. These observations are indispensable to understanding the nature and signification of Samhain.

According to the ancient Gaelic texts of Ireland, the Celtic year—at least in the British Isles, nothing being proved for the continental Celts—was divided into two equal parts, sort of like two seasons; the dark half, or winter, began on Samhain, on November 1, and the luminous half, or summer, began on Beltane, May 1. An intercalary holiday was placed in the center of each half, Imbolc on February 1 and Lugnasad on August 1. But traditionally the year began on Samhain.

This is not a hypothesis but a certitude, confirmed by the famous Coligny calendar, the sole Gallic testimony of a pre-Christian Celtic calendar. We still need to have some reservations as to its value, because not only does its existence contradict the druidic principle of refusing to write, but also it was created during the Roman era, so there is a risk that it was altered with respect to an authentically Celtic tradition. Furthermore, if we compare this calendar with what is known of the Irish calendar during the High Middle Ages, we can only be disappointed: in fact, only in November does the Gallic *(Samonios)* correspond to the Gaelic *(Samhain)*. The names of the other months of this Gallic calendar

---

*Something of this remains in English vocabulary, wherein the word *fortnight*, designating a half-month, in reality means "fourteen nights."

are completely different from those used in medieval Ireland, which are still used in the Gaelic language today.

If absolutely necessary, we can also see *Samhain* in the Gaelic name for the month of June, *Meitheamh* (Welsh *Mehefin*, Armorican Breton *Mezheven*), which derives from the older *medio-samonios* (middle of summer). The names of all the other months of the year in contemporary Gaelic have been borrowed from Latin (*Eanair*, January; *Feabhra*, February; *Marta*, March; *Abran*, April; and *Iul*, July); are periphrastic, such as *Mean Fonhair* (September— "middle of autumn"), *Deire Fomhair* (October—"end of autumn"), and *Mi na Nodlag* (December—"month of Christmas"); or are the names of ancient Celtic festivals, as in *Beltane* (May) and *Lunasa* (August). It is obvious that these terms have nothing in common with the Coligny calendar, in which *Riuros* stands for January; *Anagantios*, February; *Ogronios*, March; *Cutios*, April; *Giamonios*, May; *Simivisonnos*, June; *Equos*, July; *Elembivios*, August; *Edrinios*, September; *Cantlos*, October; and after *Samonios*, *Dumannios*, December.

The word *Samhain* in contemporary Gaelic, designating the month of November, can only be reminiscent of the ancient druidic holiday celebrated at the beginning of the lunar month, on the night of the full moon falling closest to November 1. When it concerns All Saints' Day, that is, November 1, one would say *Lâ Samhna*, "day of Samhain." The name of the day itself, during an era when orthography had not yet been fixed, took different forms, including *Samhain*, *Samain*, *Samhuin*, and even *Samfuin*. There is nothing equivocal about its definition, however: it is "the weakening of summer" or "the end of summer." And in northwestern Europe, which is subject to a gentle, humid ocean climate, and where there are only two basic seasons, summer and winter, etymology conforms with the calendrical reality. In Armorican Brittany, one enters what are called the "black months" on Toussaint (All Saints' Day), these black months being *mis du*, November (literally, "black month") and *mis kerzu*, December (literally, "very black month").

The dating of Samhain goes back to the earliest prehistory of the Celts and triggers a possible and plausible explanation for the choice of this calendrical placement, although it cannot be justified, at least by the information we currently have available to us. In fact, the entrance into the "black months" effectively signals a change in the rhythm of daily life. Because of the gentle and pleasant climate in summer, the herds can be left in their pastures. But when a certain chill begins to be felt in the air and grass becomes less abundant in the fields, it is necessary to bring the flocks back to the stables and protect them during the winter months. This is true for every pastoral society in which all material wealth is measured in the flocks.

The study of the laws and customs of the Celtic peoples, notably those of Paleo-Christian Ireland, on which we have a great deal of information at our disposal, proves that Celtic society was originally pastoral in nature. The Celts, all peoples commingled, were first nomadic shepherds who gradually, at least on the Continent, settled on rich lands that they cultivated and improved, developing at the same time the techniques of agriculture, namely through the invention of the iron plowshare and a kind of reaper-thresher, like the one displayed in the Treves Museum in Germany. During the time of Caesar, Gaul, like Sicily, was a veritable granary, and Gallic bread was renowned for its high quality.

But while the Gauls became agriculturists, or rather farmers, meaning to say that they both raised livestock and practiced agriculture, such was not the case in Ireland during the same era and for a long period afterward. Even today Ireland is primarily a country of livestock raising. This implies a long pastoral tradition, which can be reconstructed from social structures, such as those appearing in the more or less judicial or technical treatises as well as in the epic tales of the Gaelic domain.

Having long remained outside the continental tempests, and having never been integrated into the Roman Empire, Ireland in fact forms an authentic conservatory of archaic customs and traditions that can plunge one into a very remote past. It is first the existence of small, independent kingdoms, or "tribes" *(tuatha),* that are the heirs of the nomadic shepherd families of yesteryear; each time said families moved about with their herds in search of good pasturage, they ran the risk of violent confrontations with other tribes also in search of pasturage. This explains fairly well the perpetual and bloody struggles that shook Ireland throughout the Middle Ages and the lack of unity that is the fundamental characteristic of any group of Celtic origin. This "anarchy" has certainly led the Celtic peoples to be placed under the yoke of much more unified adversaries such as the Romans, the Vikings, the Anglo-Saxons, and later the Anglo-Normans. It may be considered their congenital weakness. But it also constitutes an extraordinary attempt to create a society that is more just, more responsible, and finally more egalitarian.[3]

Without going into detail, it is enough to recall the broad outlines of the very distinctive vision the Celtic peoples have of the extremely delicate relations between the collective and the individual. These relations never seem antagonistic, as is the case for the postindustrial societies that emerged in the nineteenth century. They rest on the recognition of the rights and duties of an individual within a group, in full awareness of reciprocal responsibilities, and especially in the awareness that one can be both singular and a complete member of a community.*

In ancient Celtic society property was not individually held but collective, contrary to what was the norm in Rome, where the paterfamilias was the absolute titular head of the family's belongings. Furthermore, why possess lands? An old Irish adage declares that "the kingdom extends as far as the king can see," acknowledging that the lands belong to those who occupy them as an entire community. It also recognizes that it is up to the king—the person who ensures the balance in society, who is the guarantor of contracts and the guarantor of the division of goods among all the members of the community—to protect or expand the grasslands as necessary for the herds to prosper, as these herds are the almost unique source of well-being for the tribe for whom he is responsible.

---

*In the nineteenth century, only the utopian socialist Charles-Louis Fourier defined the essentials of this conception of life in his theories on "phalanstery" and what he called "elective affinities."

There are thus no borders to the kingdom or the tribe save those defined by the extent to which the power of the king (or the small clan leader, not to mention "kinglet") may be exercised, which singularly limits, furthermore, his field of action and puts him in confrontation with other individuals of his rank ready to fight him for the survival of their own tribe. But the king (or the kinglet, the head of the clan) cannot do everything. He thus delegates some of his powers to those individuals he deems capable of assuming the missions with which he entrusts them, according to their competence and personal qualities. This is not to imply that the "delegate" would be the owner of a flock or a pasture; this delegate is in fact only a *manager,* and as such he must provide an account of his administration to his fellow citizens as well as to the king himself, who is charged with ensuring the balance among all the members of the society.

This is how a veritable "livestock contract" was established in ancient Ireland: the king entrusted a member of the tribe with the care of a herd and gave him the responsibility of parceling out the herd's production among the entire community. There are certainly quite a number of other kinds of contracts in archaic Celtic society, as the Gaelic texts portray it. There is the smith's contract, which concerns the essential master of metalwork and technological evolution; the contract with the warrior, without whom the king would be powerless in the face of any potential enemy; and the swineherd's contract, concerning the person responsible for the herds of pigs, the essential meat food of the Celtic people. There was also the contract for the harvester of barley, the cereal grain that was indispensable for the brewing of beer and its corollary, whiskey. Another was the contract for the beekeeper, who was responsible for the production of honey, a necessary element for the brewing of mead, the beverage of immortality, as well as for the baking of bread, flat cakes, or porridges, the sole vegetable foods consumed during this era.

It must be stated that the principal food of the Gaels, and of all the Celts, was milk and milk products, in the form not of cheeses (the technique of cheese making such as it is practiced today was not only unknown to them but also impossible in their overly humid country) but of curdled milk (naturally soured milk, the equivalent of yogurt or sweet milk, which is obtained thanks to rennet) and, of course, butter. When the cows no longer gave milk, they were slaughtered and their meat eaten. The meat was boiled, not roasted, according to the Celtic custom, which has survived in the British Isles, to the great despair of those dwelling on the Continent but to the great satisfaction of the adepts of a diet called—sometimes improperly—"natural."

But the raising of cattle, while it remained the essential economic activity of the Gaels of Ireland, and probably of all Celtic peoples originally, was accompanied by the raising of herds of pigs, which created wealth in almost equal proportion to the herds of cattle. The fourth branch of the Welsh mythological cycle, gathered together under the general and necessarily artificial denomination of the *Mabinogion,* makes a point of noting the appearance of pigs in the daily life of the British, who did not know this "domestic" animal and were still engaged in those "wild boar hunts" so dear to Astérix and Obélix.* The pig, in comparison to the wild boar, is a source of prodigious wealth; the domestication of wild pigs, otherwise known as boars, which people were formerly restricted to hunting, changed the lives of the Celts and allowed them to ensure their sustenance over the long centuries. It is this memory that carries the story of the fourth branch of the Welsh *Mabinogion* along. It is centered on the intervention of the magician Gwyddion, a sort of demiurge who transmitted divine secrets, in the appropriation of this domestic pig. But the Gaelic tradition of Ireland did not stop with this story, as it also gives us a Feast of Immortality, during which there is an abundant consumption of pig meat, which procures immortality for the Tuatha de Danann, the gods of pre-Christian Ireland. When defeated by the Sons of Milhead at the Battle of Tailtiu, they were forced to share the land of Ireland with their vanquishers and took refuge in the

---

*Astérix of Gaul is a very popular and long-lived cartoon series in France. —*Trans.*

underground mounds (in other words, the megalithic monuments) that tradition calls the world of the *sidh*.

A shepherd people, raising cattle for milk products and meat, and raising pigs, a food favorable for procuring immortality—such are the Celts, or, at least, such are the Gaels of Ireland, the Celtic people who have most authentically preserved their original traditions.

Under these conditions, one cannot help but comprehend the dating of this people's principal holiday on the full moon closest to November 1. This is the end of summer, when it becomes important to protect the herds—of cattle or of pigs—that constitute not only the wealth but also the survival of the community. After the storing of the summer harvest, after making provision for hay and various commodities, the herds were returned to the shelters and the people were given a share of the provisions they had gathered in order to be ready to spend the black months in the best conditions. In the stables, the cows still provided milk and the pigs furnished an almost inexhaustible source of food, as is demonstrated by the legend according to which the pigs of the "god" Mananann (who presided over the famous Feast of Immortality of the Tuatha de Danann) are killed in the evening and reborn in full health the next morning.

Legends, of course . . . But legends, which in the etymological sense are *what one should pass on,* are only the symbols of a traditional truth transported from one generation to the next. And these legends always rest on a reality whose profound meaning is no longer understood because we no longer possess the access code. There is, however, one fact for certain: within the framework of an essentially pastoral society, the holiday of Halloween, heir of the Celtic Samhain, is perfectly at home in the calendar at the end of the summer and the beginning of winter, in the specific neighborhood of November 1.

✢ The Rituals of Samhain

Irish epic and mythological tales supply abundant detail on the unfolding of the Samhain holiday, but too often these details are presented in a disorderly fashion—sometimes out of context, and sometimes even in contradiction. So it is for the duration of the holiday. In principle the holiday concerns the night of Samhain, the symbolic night that we obviously find again in the celebration of Halloween, which begins at sunset on October 31. The actual duration of the holiday, however, varies according to the texts. We will thereby say "the three days of Samhain," or rather "the three nights of Samhain," and we will then note that this deduction strictly corresponds to a brief clue collected from the Gallic calendar of Coligny, to wit, the inscription—altered but restored— *Trinous[tion] samon[i] sindiv[os]*, which may be translated as "the three nights of Samhain begin today."[4] But there is also mention in certain tales of the three days before Samhain and the three days after Samhain, which comes down to saying that this holiday lasted for seven days.

Whatever its actual duration may have been, Samhain indubitably appears to have been a "holiday of obligation" in the Christian sense of the expression, but with a reinforced value. The tale "The Birth of Conchobar," after having mentioned the "three nights before" and the "three nights after," presents the king of Ulster in his fortress of Emain Macha himself serving the guests, who were quite numerous, because "any Ulsterman who did not come on Samhain night to Emain would lose his reason and his tumulus, his tomb, and his stone would be erected the following morning."*

This clue is a valuable one: there is an obligation for all men— and also all women—belonging to the tribe, whatever their social status. Other texts prove it: "no king comes without his queen, no chief without his wife, no warrior without . . . , there comes no plebian without his concubine, nor an innkeeper without his companion, nor a boy without his beloved, nor a girl without her lover,

---

*Translation, Christian Guyonvarc'h, *Ogam*, vol. 10, p. 61. The tumulus, or mound, designates a hillock built of earth and stones; the tomb is the coffer containing the deceased; and the stone is a pillar erected next to the mound, with an inscription generally in *ogam* characters.

nor a man without his art."[5] While in these festivities, which extended beyond measure—symbolically "three days and three nights"—a very strict hierarchy was observed for the placement of each person and the food and beverages served to the various participants, and while the women generally observed the holiday in another chamber, all the members of the community— whether a kingdom or a simple tribe—were present around their king during the celebration of Samhain.[6]

What is remarkable is the inexorable punishment inflicted on those who abstained from participating in the Samhain holiday: they went mad and died. This goes much further than the Christian sanction for missing the mass on an obligatory holiday, which constitutes a sin; a person can always be given an allowance for a sin. This is not the case for the failure to celebrate Samhain. And the punishment inflicted comes not from a judgment pronounced by men but from a divine and unsparing higher power. It is obvious that this "prohibition" is of the same nature as the famous geis that underpins the individual and collective life of the ancient Gaels. *Geis,* a term related to the word *guth,* "word," is properly untranslatable (if strictly necessary we could use the word *taboo,* if its Polynesian connotations were not so strong), though it could be broadly translated as a "constraining magical incantation," an absolute obligation that could be contravened only under pain of illness, death, or dishonor (but dishonor, in any case, leads straight to illness and death). No one, whether the king, the druid, or even the most insignificant warrior or the least of shepherds, could escape the terrible geis.[7]

The religious character of Samhain is clearly apparent in this obligation, but it is a question of an era in which the distinction between the religious and the laic, between the sacred and the profane, did not exist. Samhain is also a political, legislative, judicial, and of course "commercial" festival inasmuch as contracts of all kinds were formally concluded then. Keating, a twelfth-century historian who compiled in his *General History of Ireland* all the information he could gather on the origins of the Gaels, is very explicit on this subject: "The feast of Tara was a royal and general assembly like a parliament. All the scholars of Ireland met every three years at Tara during the time of Samhain, in order to regulate and renew the rules and laws, and to approve the annals and archives of Ireland."

Samhain was also a military festival: "A throne was prepared there for each chief who commanded soldiers in the service of the king or lords of Ireland." Everything proceeded in an atmosphere of respect for a strict hierarchy, because "a throne was also prepared there for each noble of Ireland according to his rank and his function." But the discipline observed during this Samhain assembly was unsparing: "It was the custom to put to death anyone who committed violence or rape, who assaulted someone, or who made use of their weapons." In short, people were asked to leave their weapons in the vestiary: the time of Samhain was a pause during which all conflict had to be set aside, if not settled. Any who contravened this law for the slightest bellicose impulse paid with his or her life, "the king alone having the power, and no one else, to pardon such an action."

But there is no holiday, no matter what its nature, that does not include merrymaking: "They customarily spent six days drinking together before the holding of the royal assembly, which is to say three days before Samhain and three days after, concluding peace and establishing bonds of friendship between them."[8] There was thus a pacifist, somewhat fraternal element, as if an ideal society had been established for the duration of Samhain. It was then that the concept of "communion," which can be quite obviously seen reappearing in the Christian All Saints' Day, appeared.

Now communion is essentially displayed by the sharing of food and drink, exactly as in the Christian Last Supper—and also at the heart of the mysterious ritual of Eleusis in honor of the mother goddess. But this communion seems to be pushed to the extreme here, notably through the excessive consumption of alcoholic beverages. The strange tale entitled "The Drunkenness of the Ulates" bears witness to this. Conchobar, the king of Ulster, is presiding over the feast of Samhain in his fortress of Emain Macha. "Festival mead was served, one hundred tubs for each drink. The officers of

Conchobar's house said that all the nobles of Ulster would not be too many to attend this festival to the end, so great was its quality and abundance." The rest of the story obviously depicts the Ulates as being completely drunk; they have to go spend the night in the fortress of the hero Cuchulain, where he has invited them to celebrate, and so their journey across Ireland becomes a bewildering bit of errantry in the course of which they undergo the worst kinds of adventures.[9]

One would be wrong—and yet this has often been the case—to consider these drinking binges from a caricatured point of view, using the same opportunity to denounce the "puerile" nature of these boastful—and lecherous— Gauls, inveterate drunkards who, once inflamed by alcohol, squabble over petty matters and come to blows over them like real savages. It is true that the Celts—both of the Isles and of the Continent—were—and still are—fans of strong drink, but the descriptions provided of these "drinking binges" are in reality symbolic transpositions of a lived reality. We can thus declare that these Samhain feasts, which end in general drunkenness, are primarily *orgies* in the exact sense of the word, which is to say the "collective exaltation of energy," that potential energy that resides in every individual and sometimes needs to find expression through recourse to more or less magical rituals. There is a tendency to consider the orgy to be a manifestation of degeneration, even an aberrational slide into "the hell of vice" and total debauchery. Certainly the contemporary examples of various orgies—sexual "daisy chains" and other rave parties—are rather distressing in their mediocrity and vulgarity, but they still testify to an unconscious search, by debatable means, for the higher state to which all human beings aspire. The orgy is a sacred ritual whose objective has unfortunately been forgotten: to surpass the human condition by awakening all the resources of the individual in order to reach the supernatural and the divine.

The holiday of Samhain, with its excesses, its extremes, its drunkenness, reminds us of the ancient traditions concerning the Goddess of Beginnings. This woman, whom the Irish Gaels often called Medb (Maeve), is the heroine of several epic and mythological tales (you cannot have one without the other) and the bitter enemy of the Ulates. In fact, her name means "drunkenness," and in all the Celtic languages, the root of this word is the same as that characterizing *middle*. To be in a state of drunkenness is to be "in the middle," thus to be on that vague border separating the real and the imaginary worlds, the visible and the invisible, the light and the shadow, the absolute and the relative, the divine and the human. In one sense the Samhain rituals provoke an "unhooking" toward somewhere else. This observation meets up again with the Christian notion of the Communion of the Saints, celebrated on November 1, in which humans are in direct contact with the world not only of God but also of all those enthroned to his right. With its procession of phantoms, Halloween is situated on the same border but in a more popular, more anecdotal fashion.

That said, it would be fitting to take our exploration of these rituals further. The obligatory participation of all the members of the community—all social classes commingled—the absolute prohibition of killing or even assaulting any participant during the course of the festival, the "communion" and drunkenness intended to channel the energy of living beings, by structuring and lumping it together—all of this forms but one of the aspects of Samhain. Looking at the customs, such as they are described in different stories, no doubt invites other considerations, if not further speculations.

The beverage distributed to the guests of the Samhain festival was incontestably alcoholic: mead, beer, and sometimes wine. This wine was quite rare and only the great kings or powerful chiefs could obtain it, as it came from southern Gaul, or even Spain or Italy, and was quite expensive. Furthermore, there was a risk of it turning during a long voyage. In the northwestern lands, one fell back on beer and mead. But among the insular Celts, beer was primarily a "barley beer," brewed from malted barley and flavored with different herbs, as hops were not cultivated in Ireland. In truth, the beer mentioned in the various tales must have been like a horribly thin wine, its best attribute being that it was able to procure exaltation and drunkenness. Mead had a greater likelihood of being better; it all depended on the ingredients—outside of the honey and water that constituted the essentials—that were added, which, in turn, depended on what was available. But mead was in some way the "beverage of the gods." Rich in alcohol, sweet and perfumed, it was the equivalent of the Greek ambrosia and the Persian *haoma*. In any event, mead was sacred, and it accentuated the religious character of the Samhain feast.

However, we must not think that the participants in the Samhain holiday did nothing but drink alcohol. They ingested a copious amount of food, which is another characteristic of the orgy as the ancients conceived of it: excess in all its forms, but exceptionally so on certain dates. Orgies were times when traditional values, if not scorned, were at least inverted, when what was forbidden became permissible, when what was permitted was forbidden, exactly like the time of Saturnalia in Rome or like Carnival in Christian Europe.

Certainly, an isolated quatrain published by Kuno Meyer appears to contradict the orgiastic character of Samhain. In fact, it makes show of a certain sobriety: "Meat, beer, nuts, *andouille**— that's what we owe to Samhain—fire of the joyful camp upon the hill—churned milk, bread, and fresh butter." But after all, even if the bread, the butter, the whey (churned milk, which is called *lait Ribot* in Amorican Brittany), as well as the andouille and the nuts (just freshly harvested), which are foods specific to the Celts, are clearly mentioned, the quatrain makes no mention of the quantity and does not specify what meat is being consumed.

Now by all the evidence, this meat is pork (or wild boar). Even during the Christian era, pork meat was considered a sacred, if not magical, food. In the *Life of Saint Colomcille,* written in the seventh century by one of his successors at the Iona Monastery, it is attested that large herds of pigs were fattened during the fall to be slaughtered at the beginning of winter. And what about the ritual pig sacrifices that endured throughout all of western Europe, such as those contemporary rural feasts that accompany the slaughter-

---

*A pork sausage made from chitterlings.—*Trans.*

ing of the pig during the month of October, those "grog" and boudin* festivals? These rituals seem to have been inherited from the dawn of time.

One of humanity's primordial concerns has been survival: in other words, finding enough to eat in the best—or the least worst—conditions. The Celtic epics, whose original structure gives a clear idea of ancestral realities, which are not always very well understood, sketch in this regard the highlights of an evolution that was both material and spiritual. We know that Irish stories can be divided into three cycles. The first—and this is truly its place, although its tales and manuscripts are the most recent—to wit, the cycle known as the Ossian cycle or the cycle of Finn, plunges its roots into the Paleolithic Ice Age, when humans hunted reindeer to survive. The entire history of Finn Mac Cool and his son Oisin (Ossian) is, in fact, centered on the theme of the Cervidae whose name they bore and which they hunted.† This is a matter not only of an actual condition but also of a worship devoted to the Cervidae, a worship that is maintained—more or less unconsciously—in the practice of hunting: a veritable ritual sacrifice of a stag. The second cycle, that of Ulster, is, on the other hand, centered on raising cattle, the sole wealth of the tribes and the sole food available in abundance, whether as meat or as dairy products, which obviously has in corollary a kind of worship of the divine bull.[10] The third cycle, known as the "cycle of kings," represents an evolution, for it clearly evokes the appearance of the domesticated pig, which was considered a divine food because it had the potential to procure immortality. The tale "Mac Datho's Pig" testifies to this.[11] And we mustn't forget the fairy people, the Tuatha de Danann, who, after finding shelter in the world of the sidh, preserved their immortality by

---

Boudin is blood sausage. —*Trans.*

†Finn Mac Cool's real name is Finnis Demne (the hart); for half the year his wife Sabv takes the shape of a doe; the name of his son Oisin means "the fawn," and that of his grandson Oscar means "he who loves the stags." See J. Markale, *Les Triomphes du roi errant*, vol. 4 of *La Grande Epopée des Celtes* (Paris: Pygmalion, 1998). See also "The Finn Cycle" in J. Markale, *The Epics of Celtic Ireland: Ancient Tales of Mystery and Magic* (Rochester, Vt.: Inner Traditions, 2000).

consuming the flesh of "Mananann's pigs," animals that were killed in the evening but reborn on the following morning.

At first glance this sacralization of pork appears quite strange. It is certainly true that for a long time the Celts, including the Gaels, the Britons, and the Gauls, hunted wild boar, which was a very abundant game in all the forests of the British Isles and the Continent. The elements of a wild boar myth are easily found in Celtic tradition, in which this animal is usually represented as a kind of dreadful and destructive deity. In the Ossian cycle, for example, there is the monstrous boar of Ben Bulben, hunted and killed—but not without pain—by the Fiana (the troop of warrior-hunters led by Finn), Oisin, and Oscar; the boar is, incidentally, the cause of the death of the hero Diarmaid.[12] And Finn himself had the opportunity to confront a somewhat infernal wild sow in his youth. The Welsh tradition, meanwhile, describes with an extraordinary wealth of detail the hunt of the wild boar Twrch Trwyth, pursued by King Arthur and his knights.[13] It is quite obvious that the wild boar in these tales is considered an animal of the Other World, but one that is particularly malefic.

In contrast, the domestic pig is considered quite a beneficial beast. Yet it, too, is an animal of the Other World. This tradition is preserved in two of the tales that make up the Welsh *Mabinogion*. In the first branch of the *Mabinogion*, in a tale entitled "Pwyll, Prince of Dyved," we see King Pwyll, future husband of the great goddess Rhiannon, bring back a herd of pigs from the mysterious land of Arawn, following some strange adventures. These animals had been unknown on the surface of the earth before this. In the fourth branch of the *Mabinogion*, in a tale entitled "Math, Son of Mathonwy," these pigs—which are presented as exceptional animals—have become the property of Pryderi, the son of Pwyll and the king of Dyved, a country in the south of Wales. They are then stolen from him by the druid-magician Gwyddion, to the great satisfaction of the people of the kingdom of Gwyned, a country in northwestern Wales.[14]

Another story, Irish in this instance, and probably quite archaic despite the conflict between Christianity and the ancient druidic religion it evokes, strongly stresses the mythical nature of the pig. In search of vengeance against the king Muirchertach, a fairy woman named Sin, who belongs to the race of the Tuatha de Danann, enslaves and enchants the king not only through her physical charms but also by her all powerful magic. "The king pointed toward the waters of the Boyne and urged her to change them into wine. She had three casks filled from the river, cast a spell over them, and it seemed to the king and his companions that they had never tasted a more delectable wine. . . . Then she picked some ferns and turned them into pigs which like the wine the warriors partook until they were sated." Following this, the young woman promises the men she will supply them with pigs in perpetuity.[15]

The sacralization of the pig and the traditions concerning the magical, fairylike, or divine origins of this animal—essential for ensuring the feeding of a family or a tribe during the winter months (in other words, after Samhain)—explain the importance of a character who is somewhat belittled today: the swineherd. In all Celtic tales and those essentially inspired by them, the swineherd is an important dignitary, a great nobleman who is, if not the actual daily guardian of the herd, at least the person responsible for its prosperity. Furthermore, quite often these swineherds are actually druids—that is, the "gods," according to the religious concepts of the Celts. This is the case with the two swineherds Rucht and Friuch, both members of the Tuatha de Danann, one responsible for the herds of the north, the other, the herds of the south, who performed magical feats to assert their superiority.[16] And the famous Tristan, lover of Iseult, was, according to one of the *Triads of the British Isles,* the swineherd of his uncle, King Mark. It is said that King Arthur sought to make off with his herd, but Tristan saw through his ruse, to the king's great confusion.*

The meat of the pig was considered by the ancient Celts to be a food through which one could obtain immortality. Its consump-

---

*It is also claimed that the future saint Patrick, when he was captured by the Irish and made a slave of an Ulster druid, was given the responsibility of helping to guard a herd of pigs.

tion, tied to the ingestion of alcoholic drinks, essentially beer and mead, procured the drunkenness necessary for "unhooking" one-self toward the Other World. This unhooking could occur within the atemporal space of the Samhain holiday, when the Feast of the Gods is realized on the earth in a way that is not only symbolic but also magical and ecstatic. It must be noted, following through on this subject in depth, that the Christian communion, during which one shares bread and wine (the blood and flesh of Christ), is hardly different from this druidic ritual, as it too provides eternal life to those receiving it.

But among the Christians, the presence presiding over the feast of eternity is the Trinitarian god. Who plays this role for the Celts? Who presides over the holiday of Samhain? We know that in reality what is called the Celtic pantheon is only the concrete and picturesque representation of the various functions attributed to a unique deity who is invisible, ineffable, and in the final analysis unnameable. However, the study of this pantheon, through Irish stories as well as Gallo-Roman inscriptions and Greek and Roman writings, allows us to single out a remarkable character, in this instance Lugh of the Long Arm, the Master of All the Arts, he who held all the functions attributed to the deity in himself. Lugh is Pan-Celtic and has left his name on numerous cities of Celtic origin, such as Lyon, Loudon, Laon, Leyden, Leipzig, and even Carlisle on the isle of Britain, which are all "fortresses of Lugh" (Lugudunum, a name translated into Caer Lug for Carlisle). It is this same Lugh that Caesar incorporated into the Roman Mercury; Caesar said in the *De Bello Gallico* that Lugh was the most honored deity in Gaul, given the impressive number of simulacra dedicated to him in every region.

We also know that the Gallo-Roman style was to stick a Latinized Gallic name—or rather a nickname—on a Roman deity. Accordingly we find Mars Teutatis, "Mars, Father of the People," or even Apollo Grannus, "Solar Apollo." It so happens that one inscription makes mention of a certain Mercurius Moccus, or "Mercury Pig." This takes us back to a strange Breton legend, which has a heavy Christian influence, of the demon Huccan, whose name means "little pig," and who is portrayed as a diabolic version of the ancient god Lugh.[17] So it seems quite probable that it was Lugh of the Long Arm, the Master of All the Arts, the victor in the Battle of Mag Tured against the dark and destructive powers, the Fomor, who presided over the Feast of Immortality of Samhain.[18]

Lugh is a civilizing god, a god of light who fights the powers of the shadow. His name is, in fact, connected to the Indo-European root word that is expressive of whiteness and sparkling brightness. This is to say that Samhain, though it marks the end of the summer months and the entrance into the "black months," is a holiday of light, which is not belied by the understanding of the Christian All Saints' Day as an exaltation of the "world of light," or Paradise. And fire properly plays a role in the Samhain rituals. It was Keating who confirmed this in his *General History of Ireland,* as he describes the institution of sacrificial fires during the night of Samhain; he specifies that it "was obligatory, under penalty of fine, to extinguish all the fires in Ireland on that night." This is obviously reminiscent of what happens during Paschal Week in Christian liturgy. The flames burning in churches are extinguished on Black Friday, and it is necessary to wait for the Paschal service and the blessing of the new fire for them to be relit. We can also compare the sacrificial fire of Samhain with the fires of Beltane, which is celebrated on May 1. On this occasion it is the high king of Ireland who lights the first fire, and no one, under pain of punishment, has the right to do so before him. We can thus easily grasp the sense of this ritual: the past year is extinguished symbolically, it is plunged into darkness, and it is the druids—or the gods—who open the new year by lighting a fire on which a sacred virtue has been conferred, a spiritual fire thanks to which human beings, during this period of darkness, would be guided by the light emanating from this divine power.

But it seems that the ancient Celts celebrated another ritual at this same time that has been too rarely associated with Samhain, that of the famous "harvesting of the mistletoe." Current opinion places this harvesting around the time of Christmas, hence the well-known expression of "mistletoe on the New Year." But this dating is completely arbitrary. The sole testimony we possess on this ritual is that of Pliny the Elder, and he made absolutely no reference to the winter solstice. He was content to declare that the mistletoe had to be cut "the sixth day of the moon . . . because the moon already has considerable strength without yet being at the center of its cycle."[19] That's all. Why not assume that mistletoe, a plant sacred to the druids, was harvested during Samhain? This assumption is further reinforced by the fact that the actual gathering of mistletoe formed only part of the mistletoe ritual. It was extended, still according to Pliny, by the sacrifice of two young bulls. And this sacrifice naturally reminds one of Samhain.

✚ Death and Rebirth of the King

Here is what Pliny wrote after providing his definition of mistletoe: "After having prepared a sacrifice at the foot of a tree, two white bulls whose horns have knit for the first time are brought there." A brief description of the harvesting of the mistletoe follows. Then the druids "immolated the victims while imploring the deity to make this sacrifice a profitable one for those to whom it was offered." Unfortunately, Pliny does not tell us what deity this sacrifice is intended for nor to whose profit it was performed, and it is only by comparison with Irish texts that we are able to find this shred of information. In the tale "The Illness of Cuchulain," the men of Ireland have gathered together at Tara to choose a king: "They then organized the feast of the bull to know by this means to whom they would give the kingship. The feast of the bull is performed in this way, which is to say a white bull is killed; one lone man must eat to repletion of its meat and broth and sleep upon this repletion, and four druids chant a word of truth* over him. He would see within his dream the guise of the man who should be elevated to the crown by his appearance, by his character, by his

*A magical spell.

bearing, and the work he does."* Another text, *The Birth of Conare the Great*, is even more explicit: "A bull was killed and it was put in a large caldron to cook. A man was then chosen to eat the meat of this bull and to drink the broth it was cooked in before going to sleep in one of the houses of Tara. Magical incantations were spoken over him and he slept. The one he saw in his dream should be the future king. The next morning, he had to recount all that he had seen but if he should lie his lips withered. This was the Feast of the Bull at Tara of the Kings."†

Having reached this point in our examination of Samhain, it is impossible not to mention a later text, dating from the end of the twelfth century, written by a Welsh cleric named Giraldus Cambrensis on the instigation of King Henry II Plantagenet, who had just, as we know from our history lessons, taken possession of Ireland. The work is entitled *Topographia Hibernica*, and it includes valuable information on the mores and customs of Gaelic Ireland at the time of the arrival of the Anglo-Normans. However, as with all propagandistic compositions (of which this is certainly one), it is important to examine it prudently.

Giraldus Cambrensis reported, speaking of one populace of Ulster, that they were "accustomed, by a rite which was more than barbaric and abominable, to give themselves a king by the following manner. The entire populace would assemble in a chosen location, a white mare would be brought into the midst of the assembly and he [the future king] was intended to be raised to the dignity not of a prince but a beast, and would conduct himself with that mare as if he were an animal. This beast would be killed shortly thereafter.

---

*Translation, Christian Guyonvarc'h, *Ogam*, vol. 10, p. 293. With all due deference to the translator, who stubbornly refuses all non-Indo-European influence upon the Celtic tradition, it certainly seems that the custom described here would be similar to the ecstatic ritual of the Asian shamans indexed so well by Mircea Eliade in his work, which is too important to be overlooked: *Shamanism*, 2nd ed. (Princeton: Princeton/Bollingen, 1972).

†Markale, *Les Seigneurs de la brume*, p. 54. Other tales featuring the king Conare as hero present different forms of rituals for the choice and enthronement of the king; ibid., p. 54.

It was cut into pieces and boiled in water, then that broth was used to prepare a bath. The future king would immerse himself therein, eat the pieces of meat presented to him, surrounded by his people who ate alongside him. He drank the broth in which he bathed not with a container, nor even with his hand, but with his mouth. When he had performed this rite, his sovereignty and authority was consecrated."[20]

It was in the complete interest of Giraldus Cambrensis to blacken the picture he painted of Ireland to the greater advantage of his patron, Henry Plantagenet, who could thus justify his iron grip on these barbarians and *untermenschen,* as was said of these alleged "sub-races" during the Nazi era. But even though he obligingly added details, it does not mean his description of twelfth-century Ireland is totally devoid of interest. There is never smoke without fire. This solemn enthronement of the king of the tribe of Ulster demonstrates that Gaelic society at the time of the Anglo-Norman conquest retained some strongly archaic structures, something confirmed by the epic and mythological tales transcribed during that era, in particular the famous *Leabhar Gabala* (Book of Conquests), a learned compilation of ancient oral traditions or earlier manuscripts.

That said, while displaying all his horror and disapprobation, the Welsh cleric appears to have comprehended nothing of the ritual he described. This incomprehension is responsible for an improper interpretation of the enthronement of the king of Ireland through comparing it with the Indian practice of *ashvamedha.*

In India, the ceremony known as ashvamedha takes place in the following manner: After selecting a stallion of good breeding and fine form, and after having let it wander freely where it would (but under the strict surveillance of the collective), the people presented it to the queen, who would couple with it. Then the horse would be killed. There can be no doubt as to the meaning behind the ashvamedha; it is a fertility rite by which the queen is impregnated—symbolically—by the animal and procures for the people, of whom she is sovereign, the results of that unusual impregnation, meaning the collective prosperity. In the ritual described by Giraldus Cambrensis, everything is reversed: the king supposedly impregnates the mare, but the mare is then killed, which seems, to speak bluntly, to be pure stupidity. In this specific case there is not the slightest trace of a fertility rite. As Georges Dumézil writes, "If we imagine that, in imitation of ashvamedha, the dead horse . . . would supposedly impregnate a woman who remained living, the more unlikely is the idea that the king claims to impregnate a mare who is, immediately after the act, not only killed, but cut into pieces and eaten."[21] The argument is irrefutable.

There is more. Giraldus Cambrensis wrote in Latin, in medieval Latin, to be precise. It so happens that his words *candidum jumentum* prompted the simplistic translation "white mare." Now, in this dog Latin of the twelfth century, *jumentum* carried the meaning of "beast of burden." So the term would also be perfectly appropriate for bovines, for example, a cow, cattle having greatly served Western peasants as well as insular Celts over the course of the centuries as draft animals and beasts of burden. Most important, we should remember that as a general rule all the Celts, but particularly the insular Celts, refused to eat the meat of horses.* Both sides have made their case: what Giraldus Cambrensis described is a ceremony of royal enthronement during which a bull—or a cow—considered sacred was sacrificed; the animal's death, if agreeable to the deity, prompted the divine blessing over the herds of cattle that formed the sole true wealth of these people. We have come back to those structures of Celtic society that are incontestably of pastoral origin. As for the bull, as we know well, it is the symbol of martial activity with an eye to ensuring collective prosperity for numerous groups. The sacrifice of the bull, an animal precious to the deity, is therefore not a fertility rite but a ritual through which the people hope to earn the deity's beneficial influence.

---

*Even at the present date there is no hippophagous butchery in Ireland, and a great debate is raging among the Irish, who are great breeders of racehorses, as the world knows, but who are faced by European Union regulations obliging them to export for butchering any animals that are hurt or too old. Is there a trace of ancient totemism in this? It is a cold fact, and it helps us understand how Giraldus Cambrensis's "white mare" resulted from a misinterpretation—and even in defiance of common sense.

We can also put forth another hypothesis concerning the bull sacrifice if we regard the bull as a substitute victim. The biblical story of Isaac is a well-known example of this. Could it be the same in the story told by Giraldus Cambrensis? Couldn't the beast of burden sacrificed be a substitute for the king himself?

The question is worth examining, especially in relation to the numerous Irish epics in which a king, for different reasons, generally because he has contravened his *gessa*, which is to say his functional prohibitions, falls under the blows of his enemies, or even his friends. The most characteristic case is that of Conare the Great. His gessa are strange, but no doubt we do not know their exact meaning: "You will not travel around the fortress of Tara by the right, nor the plain of Berg by the left; you must never hunt the wild animals in the Cerna Valley; you will not go outside of Tara on the ninth night of every month; you will not sleep in a house where the fire is still lit and where the gleam of the hearth is visible from outside; you cannot leave this house after sunset; you must never see before you three men dressed in red; no theft should be committed in your kingdom while you rule; you will not allow any man to enter the house you are in after sunset; you must never settle a quarrel between two of your servants, personally."[22]

If we understand this correctly, the major prohibition is that *no theft must be committed under his reign,* because the king is not only the distributor of wealth among all the members of the community but also the guarantor of the balance and harmony of all. This harmony cannot tolerate any injustice, and the Celtic version of a king, who is not an absolute monarch, must account for his actions before the members of his tribe. He enjoys no immunity, and if they are not satisfied with him, he may be eliminated and another chosen to take his place.

Now in the case of Conare, he personally settles a quarrel between two of his servitors. This is a fatal transgression: *there should not be any quarrel,* and if there is one, it is the king's fault. He is guilty. In immediate succession he contravenes all his other prohibitions and dies, on the night of Samhain, during an unlikely battle whose various episodes are so many symbolic elements inherited from the oldest mythology.[23] It can be said that what we have here is the detailed description of an actual ceremony, obeying precise rituals leading to the sacrificial murder of the king.

The same is true for the king Muirchertach, son of Erca. Seduced by the fairy Sin, he neglects not only his legitimate wife and children but also all of his people. He is thus guilty of negligence. The instrument of the justice enacted against him is a being from the Other World, the mysterious Sin. This shows that the invisible powers intervene, essentially during the period of Samhain, in human affairs and that they are in some way the "conscience" that watches over the harmony of the world.

In fact, the sacrifice of King Muirchertach takes place over a period of time that is indeterminate but that, in context, corresponds to the three days before and after Samhain. The young woman, Sin, whose name means "to sigh" but also "breath" and "brutal wind," surrounds the king with a series of events and perceptions that she has the power to create *ex nihilo* by virtue of her membership in the Tribes of Danann: "The king slept in a deep magical sleep provoked by Sin who, while he slept, got up and arranged all the warriors' swords and javelins in front of the doors, with their tips pointing inwards. Her art summoned numerous hosts around the fortress in which she locked herself after setting fire everywhere, upon the ramparts and the keep." The king awoke, terrified at the sound of "the crackling of a burning keep and the din, all about him, of an army of demons. . . . Not realizing that all this was an illusion and that in reality not a single soldier was besieging his fortress, Muirchertach rose in haste and sought his weapons, but found not a one. As for Sin, she rushed out of the keep, and he followed her, but he ran into some warriors at the door against whom he collided so firmly that he was pushed back toward his bed, while his enemies fled. . . . The king stepped back toward the door, but flames were now crackling and sparks flying between it and him. And when the fire had invaded the corridor and encircled the entire keep, Muirchertach no longer had any place in which to seek shelter. Grabbing a helmet filled with wine, he poured it over him as protection, but the roof collapsed on his head, and the fire burned five feet of his length, the wine protecting the rest."[24]

This hallucinatory description also brings to mind the death of King Conare, who while in the hostel of Da Derga is beseiged by his enemies and the druids, who have cast spells to dry out all the casks and all the wells of Ireland. Conare has an unquenchable thirst and will die at the hands of the inner fire that consumes him.[25] Fire, real or symbolic, has its role in the sacrificial rituals of Samhain, and Keating, in his *General History of Ireland,* is not wrong to point out that the druids of Ireland "burned their victims" in the new fires they had lit during this night. What is important is knowing who these victims were. But it is probable that it was the king who played the role of victim.

Furthermore, the rite appears confused. One wonders whether the victim was suffocated (by hanging or dehydration), drowned (by the helmet filled with wine), or burned (by fire or an interior conflagration). We find the same confusion in the scholias—later, but revelatory—in the manuscript of the *Pharsalia* by the Roman poet Lucan, when he mentions the "sinister Gallic sanctuaries" lost in the depths of the forests. These scholia cite the names (or rather the epithets, the cognomens) of three Gallic deities, vouched for incidentally by numerous Gallo-Roman inscriptions—Teutas or Toutatis ("father of the people"), Esus ("good"?), and Taranis ("thunder," thus "fire from the sky")—and indicate the kind of sacrifice proper for each deity, wherein we find hanging, drowning, or death by fire again. But what we do not know precisely is whether these sacrifices were real or simulated (substitution) rituals.

Missing from these references is the severed head. Its importance has been long proved by archaeological objects discovered in the territory of ancient Gaul, the writings of various Greek and Roman historians (Diodorus Siculus and Titus Livy, mainly), Welsh and Irish stories, and the numerous Roman sculptures found in the British Isles and on the Continent. These all lend weight to the conviction that the worship of severed heads was prevalent among all the Celtic peoples.

When writing about the Battle of Clusium, between the Romans and the Gauls, after describing the events Titus Livy adds what he had learned of a Gallic custom of cutting off the heads of enemies and preserving them. "They carried these heads," he tells us, "on the breastplates of their horses."[26] This custom does not seem to have been an imaginary fantasy, for we can see in the ruins of the cities of Glanum (Saint-Rémy-de-Provence), Saint-Blaise near Istres, and Entremont, not far from Aix-en-Provence, as well as in the Borély Museum in Marseilles, pillars from the Gallic era that are "skull hangers," still equipped with their holding nails. We can also see in the Granet Museum of Aix and the Calvet Museum of Avignon Gallic sculptures predating the Roman conquest that depict severed heads, most often with their eyes closed. And on certain Gallic coins, such as those of the Osismii people (Finistère), numerous depictions of bodiless heads can be seen. Finally, in the Gallic version of the quest of the Grail, the tale of Peredur, we are presented with the sacred object in the form of a platter holding a man's severed head bathed in his own blood.[27]

But this concerns a worship whose exact significance remains obscure. We must restrict ourselves to pointing it out and no more. On the other hand, it would be fitting to give more examination to the form of ritual murder known as decapitation (that of Saint John the Baptist being the best-known example). There are three specific cases of this kind of sacrifice worth studying. The first can be found in the Gaelic tale "The Death of Curoi." This story concerns the rivalry between the hero of light, Cuchulain, and his dark double, Curoi Mac Daere, mythical king of Munster and a kind of protean infernal deity. Following some earlier quarrels, Cuchulain comes to an understanding with Curoi's wife, the young Blathnait—whom Curoi abducted from Cuchulain previously— that she would betray the king and deliver him into the hero's hands. This is done, and Cuchulain with one blow of his sword cuts through the neck of Curoi.[28] Why? Because Curoi Mac Daere did not keep his commitments and therefore became a king without power, and thus a bad king.

The second case is shown in the second branch of the Welsh *Mabinogion*, entitled *Branwen, Daughter of Llyr*. Bran Vendigeit, meaning "Bran the Blessed," has brought his men (Britons of the isle) to

Ireland to avenge the fate suffered by his sister Branwen. The Britons experience a crushing defeat, and there are no more than seven survivors in addition to Bran, whose leg is wounded. Bran asks his warriors to cut off his head and bring it with them.[29] The remaining portion of the story refers to the worship of the severed head, but the sacrificial ritual is clearly established.

In fact, Bran is not fatally wounded. He can easily heal. But he has been vanquished and is responsible for the defeat. He must pay with his life for his inability to be a king worthy of his name and duties. Oddly enough, this—legendary—story of Bran the Blessed seems to step straight out of an event—this time half historical, half legendary—that took place around 280 B.C. in Greece, during an expedition (real or imaginary?) undertaken by the Gauls under the leadership of a chief bearing the name Brennos. Brennus or Brennos is nothing other than the Latin—or Greek—transcription of Bran. In fact, it concerns the same mythological figure.* And according to the Greek historiographer Diodorus Siculus, who is generally well informed on Celtic antiquities, when the Gauls suffered a defeat in Delphi and lost several thousand men, Brennos, "himself wounded three times, called the surviving Gauls to assemble. Then speaking before them, he advised them to finish off all the wounded, burn their chariots, and quickly return to their country. He also counseled them to choose Kikorios as their leader. Then Brennos, being inebriated, stabbed himself."[30]

The religious nature of the suicides of Bran and Brennos is undeniable. It is as the individuals responsible for their troops that the two chiefs—in fact, two kings—offer themselves as expiatory victims. There is another example—entirely historical this time— of such a ritual sacrifice, that of Vercingétorix surrendering to Caesar. First we need to state explicitly that Vercingétorix made

---

*There is another more or less historical figure, the Senoni chief Brennus, who took Rome—except for the capital—in 387 B.C., who in many respects resembles Brennos of the expedition to Delphi and Bran the Blessed of the Welsh tradition. All three of their names mean "crow," but also "height" and "hill."

himself a prisoner knowing full well what kind of fate awaited him. He surrendered himself primarily because the council of Gallic chiefs had decided upon this course of action. Vercingétorix had failed in the mission with which he had been entrusted; he had to become the victim to spare his fellows a fate that could have been much grimmer. And whether or not it was of his own free will that Vercingétorix cast his arms at the feet of the Roman proconsul, he had to perform this gesture because he was—as his name clearly expresses—"the king of the great warriors."

However, the king is not always responsible for disaster, famine, or climatic conditions, or even the breakup of the society of which he is basically the "manager." We know quite well that the exercise of power is wearing, and that a king, like any political leader, loses both his credibility and authority when times go bad. This is no hypothesis but a reality proved countless times throughout human history, in all latitudes and in all eras. Wouldn't there be a correlation between this "wear and tear of power" and the fairly complex and what we must say are rather confused rituals—taking into account the obscurity of the texts and alterations due to the incomprehension of certain Christian copyists—that seem to have taken place during the period of Samhain, not only in Ireland but also in all other Celtic countries? In a word, couldn't the sacrificial death of the king be masking another ritual, one of regeneration?

To learn if this is so, we need to return to the famous scholia of Lucan, which have been the object of so much analysis, and most particularly those concerning Teutas. This is what the scholiast wrote: "Mercury Teutas is honored by the Gauls in this way: the head of a man is plunged into a great cauldron so that he suffocates."[31] This is fairly vague but quite valuable. Here Teutas, the "father of the people," is incorporated into Mercury, and not Mars, as is the case in some Gallo-Roman inscriptions. Now Mercury, we should recall, is the Gallo-Roman aspect of the Pan-Celtic Lugh, the Master of All the Arts who comprises within himself alone all the functions attributed to the deity who most likely presided over the Feast of Immortality, and who, consequently, is honored during the feast of Samhain. We are within our rights to ask what were the sources used by the scholiast Lucan concerning this suffocation ritual and whether this tradition is an ancient one or not. But it appears to be corroborated by a magnificent archaeological object that is one of the most remarkable monuments for understanding Celtic mythology. It is the famous Gundestrup Cauldron, which dates from the second century A.D. and is housed in the Aarhaus Museum in Denmark.

This cauldron is made of silver and formed from several plates carved with picturesque scenes swarming with astounding figures, in particular the Goddess of the Birds and, in a so-called Buddhist posture, the god Cernunnos of the Gauls. This imagery has always had features in common both with the tail sides of certain Gallic coins and with Welsh and Irish texts. Accordingly, when examining the rituals of Samhain with the assumption that they are structured on the theme of rebirth or at least of regeneration, one of these plates particularly compels our attention. On the right side of this plate we see three men with their heads facing left and blowing horns that are bent back in the form of horses' heads. On the lower half of this right side, a man advances toward the left with a sword over his shoulder and no shield; his helmet is decorated with a figure of a wild boar. In front of him six men march toward the left, each brandishing a spear in the right hand while holding a long shield transversely across the body with the left. They have no emblems on their helmets, but there is some kind of sun on their shields.

On the left side of the plate, over the entire upper half, an immense figure plunges an upside-down warrior into a kind of pot (no doubt a cauldron). An animal, either a dog or a wolf, can be seen beneath this pot. On the upper left half, four horsemen ride toward the right, seemingly coming from where the sacrifice is taking place. The first and third riders hold spears in their left hands. All of their helmets have designs: the first has a vague m shape, the second a horn symbol, the third a wild boar, and the fourth a bird. The horses' harnesses show flowers that look like lotuses. In front of these horsemen, a ram-headed serpent appears to be guiding them.

In between the two halves stretches a totally horizontal tree from whose top side emerge seven flowers with three petals or seven leaves with three lobes. On the lower side there are only six of these leaves or flowers. All the way over on the left, the tree has three roots that seem to originate from the cauldron.

The interpretation of this veritable symbolist painting does not appear too difficult. The warriors on the bottom half who have nothing on their helmets and are marching to the left—the traditionally and etymologically *sinister* side—are men who have been killed or wounded in combat. The large figure, perhaps Teutas, in any event one of the many aspects of the god Lugh, is dipping them into a container so as to restore their life or health. The fact that the warriors heading toward the right, this time on horseback, have a triumphal bearing and are led by the ram-headed serpent, a symbol of fertility, indicates this quite clearly. The illustration is not even lacking the Tree of Life and the flowers of immortality.

The key to this illustration resides in the container, the pot or cauldron. Celtic tradition, in Wales as well as in Ireland, makes frequent mention of it. It is first the cauldron of Bran the Blessed: "I will give you a cauldron whose virtue is this: if a man be killed today, you have naught but to cast him within so that on the following day he will be as good as ever, save that he will no longer have the power of speech."[32] A similar cauldron sends Peredur— the Welsh equivalent of Perceval—into a trance when he spies it during his stay at the Castle of the King of Suffering: "He saw a horse arrive bearing a corpse on its saddle. One of the women arose, took the corpse off the saddle, bathed it in a tub filled with warm water, which was below the gate, and applied a precious ointment to it. The man was revived, and came over to greet him with an expression of joy upon his face."[33] Of course we do not see the cauldron of rebirth only in Celtic tales. For example, the Greek poet Pindar recounts how Pelops, having been cut into pieces and boiled in a cauldron, had his limbs replaced and his life and health restored by Clotho, the deity who presides over birth.[34] To this collection we should add a number of Armorican Breton stories in which a hero or heroine—after being dismembered and boiled in a cauldron—regains his or her original integrity.*

It certainly seems that this mysterious cauldron would have a certain connection to the "holy" Grail of the Arthurian epics, especially the ones that describe this vessel as an emerald that once sat on the brow of Lucifer and fell to the earth when he was cast from Heaven into the darkness.[35] In short, the Grail possesses virtues comparable to those of the Celtic cauldron: it heals and restores life to those who gaze upon it or drink its contents—the "blood of Christ," in other words; it is the thing "that is most precious of all that is in the world." The Grail also contains an inexhaustible store of food, a source of divine nourishment. This is also the virtue of Dagda's Cauldron in the Irish tradition. "The Story of the Battle of Mag Tured" states quite clearly that "no company would go away from it empty-handed,"[36] while in the Welsh tale "Culwch and Olwen," King Arthur, to complete a sacred mission, must first take possession of the "Cauldron of Diwrnach the Gael," which also provides an inexhaustible source of food.[37] But pay heed! In his poem *The Remains of the Abyss*, the Welsh bard Taliesin notes that the cauldron "sweetly heated by the breath of nine young women . . . will not boil the food of a coward," which means that one may participate in this Feast of Immortality only if one is worthy. The same holds for those who are admitted to the famous Meal of the Grail.†

The origin of this cauldron is obviously quite mysterious but refers constantly to the Other World. The Cauldron of Dagda is said to have been transported by the tribes of the goddess Dana

---

*In many cases, however, they are missing a toe or have some small physical defect that will then play an important role, mainly one that allows the heroine to be recognized by the hero of the tale. This is the well-known theme of Queen Pédauque, the "queen with the goose foot." Journeying into the Other World often causes a physical anomaly in the person who has managed to pull off this feat and return. Several narratives of this kind can be read in J. Markale, *Contes populaires de toutes les Bretagnes* (Rennes: Éditions Ouest-France, 1977).

†See *La Naissance du roi Arthur*. According to the *Triads of the British Isles*, among the thirteen wonders of Britain is the cauldron of Tyrnog. If food is placed within it for a coward, it will not boil.

"from the isles of the North of the world," the north being one of the symbols used by the Celts to designate a mythical land or realm of Faery. Countless epics describe the fantastic adventures of heroes who enter forbidden domains to seize a sacred object they are obliged to carry away, or who are there given by a divine figure some sort of talisman that will allow them to accomplish their tasks.*

But the Other World is "everywhere and nowhere." The invisible is immediately behind the visible: it is enough to have the famous gift of "second sight" to see it. In principle, it is people who have undergone some form of initiation who possess this gift. But it can happen that on certain dates any human being has the potential to perceive the invisible world and even enter it with impunity. This is precisely what happens during the time of Samhain; countless stories emphasize this favorable relationship that allows access to the sacred and talismans from the Other World. The way in which the hero Bran the Blessed gained possession of his magical cauldron is, in this regard, quite significant.

A certain Matholwch, king of Iwerddon (Ireland), who wished to wed Bran's sister Branwen, recounted to Bran how one day while hunting on a mound overlooking a lake he saw emerging from this lake "a huge man with red hair, carrying a cauldron on his back. He was of inordinate height and had the air of an evildoer. And if he was big, his wife was two times bigger than he." These are obviously folk from the Other World, and the description of the redheaded man is quite in conformance with that of the "churl" who appears quite often in Irish stories, with his wild hair and a club in his hand. But in this instance the churl is carrying a cauldron, which, as one finds out later, restores life to the dead that are placed within it. However, this story takes on a very odd twist.

In fact, the churl and his wife remain in Matholwch's domain for a year, but "before the end of the fourth month, they speedily and

---

*The Greek historiographer Strabo reports that the Cimbrians, a Germanic people heavily influenced by the Celts, offered Emperor Augustus "that which they had most dear and precious, to wit their sacred cauldron." See Strabo, *Geography*, vol. 7 (Boston: Harvard/Loeb Classical Library, 1917), p. 2.

unrestrainedly committed a series of excesses within the land. . . . My vassals decided to build a house entirely of iron. When it was ready they had all of Iwerddon's smiths come there with hammers and tongs, and had coal piled about the house as high as the roof." The text does not say how, but we are given to understand that the red-haired man and his family were somehow obliged to enter this strange house. "They sent in an abundance of food and drink to the woman, the man, and their children. When they saw they were drunk, they set fire to the coal around the house and played the bellows upon it until everything was white hot. The family took counsel in the center of the room. The man waited there until the iron wall had turned white. As the heat had become intolerable, he gave it a blow with his shoulder and emerged, casting it aside, followed by his wife. Nobody else escaped. . . . It was then that he came here and gave me this cauldron."[38] This cauldron would be subsequently offered to Bran, to seal the accord between the two kings.

This story is told in the second branch of the Welsh *Mabinogion,* but it appears in almost identical form in the Irish tale "The Drunkenness of the Ulates." During the course of a Samhain night, King Conchobar, Cuchulain, and the Ulates leave a feast given by the king at Emain Macha to continue their banquet in Cuchulain's fortress. But because they are thoroughly intoxicated, they become lost during their journey and so end up wandering throughout Ireland. This is how they arrive before the fortress of Cruachan, residence of Ailill and Medb, king and queen of Connaught, sworn enemies of the Ulates. An old man who is somewhat of a prophet, when asked by Medb about the presence of the Ulates, answers her: "Their coming has long been foretold and some thought has been given it. Here is what must be done: prepare a house of iron between two house of wood, with an underground house below, a very hard plate of iron upon which will be piled firewood and coal so that this underground house will be completely filled with it. It has been predicted that the Ulster nobles will one night all be assembled within an iron house."[39]

The similarity is remarkable enough to provide an interesting stopping point. This story continues with the same events that occurred in the *Mabinogion.* Queen Medb decides to follow the path indicated by the prophecies. She gives a very warm welcome to the Ulates and keeps them amused while others are busy building the iron house that will be an ideal trap for ridding herself of her enemies. When is everything is in readiness, the Ulate nobles find themselves—still drunk—in the iron house, and they are brought copious portions of food and drink, which only heightens their inebriated state. But the men of Connaught then lock the door on them and attach the house to seven stone pillars with seven iron chains. Then, "three times fifty smiths were brought who stoked the fire with their bellows. They made three rings around the house and they lit the fire not only under but over the house, in such a way that the fire's heat penetrated the house."

Of course, the Ulates quickly realize the nature of the trap they have fallen into. Some of them accuse Cuchulain for having brought them there, blaming him for all ills that may befall them. The hero, vexed by these reproaches, which he deems unjustified, solemnly declares that he will do everything it takes to pull his companions out of the predicament they find themselves in. He sticks his sword in one of the walls and sees that it is made of iron. It is impossible to pierce it. He then jumps up in the air, making one of those great leaps for which he possesses the secret ability; he demolishes part of the house and eventually shakes down the entire fortress.* King Ailill, who has not yet been heard from in this chapter, then intervenes and reproaches his wife for flouting the laws of hospitality. The Ulates are led into an oak house, and they are brought beer and food. Once again, the men of Ulster are drunk, but they feel like prisoners all the same. Challenged by his companions, Cuchulain leaps and does the "leap of the salmon," one of the special tricks he learned during his sojourn with the Scottish witches. This allows him to knock off the upper half of

---

*We should not forget that the Celtic type of fortress is not the medieval castle-fort but a fortified enclosure, generally built upon a hill, inside of which different separate structures were raised. The same holds true for the Christian Celtic monasteries of the High Middle Ages.

the roof and to find himself on the roof of another house. But the essential need has been satisfied: he has freed his companions and, overall, gotten them out of the "crematory oven" in which they had been condemned to perish. An epic battle between the Ulates and the men of Connaught follows, but the Ulates emerge from it quite well. The conclusion is simple: Cuchulain has emerged alive and stronger than ever—with the companions for whom he was responsible—from the trial by fire to which he had been subjected.

There is no mention of any cauldron in the Irish narrative, but it is not impossible that it was present in the original oral tradition that was later transcribed by Christian monks. In any case, the similarities between the Welsh and Irish tales give us leave to assume so. For, as we have already seen, this cauldron is of singular importance in the Welsh text, which established a direct link between the theme of the cauldron and that of the house heated until it is white hot. The parallel is simple: in both cases, fire—which was not an element in and of itself for the Celts, but which metamorphoses the three fundamental elements of Earth, Air, and Water, as is shown by the *triskell,* the triple spiral—plays a primordial role. It is a dynamic agent, the preeminent agent of transformation that no one can do without.

The comparison arises here with the practices but especially the ideals of traditional alchemy. This is not to claim that the ancient Celts knew and practiced alchemy. It is simply a matter of establishing a parallel: the objective pursued is the same, the *transformation* if not the *transfiguration* of the being. In Welsh and Irish stories as in certain Armorican Brittany folktales,* the cauldron—which contains a divine

---

*One story, collected in the Trégor by Luzel during the nineteenth century and published by him under the title "La Perruque du roi Fortunatus," for which there are other versions in various regions of Brittany—among which is one I published under the title "Saga de Yann" in my work *La Tradition celtique en Bretagne armoricaine* (Paris: Payot, 1975)—conforms quite closely to the original outline. In fact, we see here a young man successfully pass several different, extremely dangerous initiatory tests to be condemned at the stake. But covered with an ointment provided him by a sorcerer, he emerges from the flames more alive than ever, and especially more handsome than before (pp. 166–67).

food procuring immortality for those who partake in it—and the athanor of the alchemists—in which slowly but surely a metamorphosis of raw primal matter is transformed into the purified, elaborate, and *spiritualized* Philosopher's Stone—have a definite equivalence.

The athanor and the cauldron contain something that slakes thirst and satisfies hunger. These contents are what the participants ingest during the course of a feast. The participants attain repletion concerning food, and drunkenness insofar as drink is concerned, in an authentic orgy that lets them pass from one plane of consciousness to another. In the tale from the *Mabinogion*, excess eating, intoxication, and fire are complementary elements. It is thanks to them that the redheaded man can emerge from this trial unscathed.

For the "house heated white hot" is an initiatory sacrificial ritual, with a very clear-cut relationship to Samhain, and particularly brings to mind what certain ancient authors wrote regarding human sacrifice or what they alleged to be such. The Gauls "have large mannequins with willow sides, which they fill with living men; they set them afire, and the men inside die, enveloped by the flames."[40] The scholiast of Lucan said almost exactly the same thing concerning the sacrifices to the god Taranis: "They burn a certain number of men in a wooden cage." Strabo, for his part, declares that the Gauls "manufactured a colossus out of wood and straw, then filled it with both wild and domestic animals as well as with men, then burned the entire thing."[41] Just what exactly are they talking about?

To answer this question it is necessary to go back to folk customs that have survived for centuries in the countryside. After all, the ancient holiday of Samhain is no longer celebrated, but it survives, as we have already said, in a religious form, the Christian All Saints' Day, and in a popular form, the folklike Halloween, which is unquestionably carnival-like. The mannequin mentioned by Caesar, the wooden cage in Lucan's scholiast, and Strabo's colossus are obviously comparable to the grotesque mannequin of King Carnival, which is burned following the festival. But when we get to the bottom of the issue, we see that Carnival corresponds to a symbolic reversal of values, a time in which the "excluded" become "included" and those who are normally "included" are repressed into the mob of the "excluded."

Now, for centuries both smiths and lepers were among the "excluded"—that is, those who live on the margins of society. The smiths, masters of fire, had a suspicious, subterranean, and almost demonic occupation. Society needed them, but they were feared because they knew the secrets of the earth, its minerals and that mysterious fire that growls evasively in a world of darkness. Smiths thus formed an indispensable "caste" that was accepted but distrusted, and most often they were forced to live on the outskirts of inhabited areas. As for lepers, they were driven from the community because people were scared of being contaminated by them. One similarity can be noted between lepers and smiths; in fact, a common complaint of lepers is that they suffer from an inner burning, that they are being devoured by their illness in some way until there is nothing left but a pile of ashes. Lepers therefore lived in a community, but outside of the village. However, we should take care that we are not fooled by a simplistic classification: in numerous cases, lepers, who are also called *cacous* in some regions, were not all stricken by this terrible disease. Quite often in normal rural parlance lepers were primarily marginal individuals who lived outside the norms of public life.

One may ask why lepers have come up in this examination of the rituals of the Samhain holiday. The answer is simple, but it derives from a fairly subtle bit of reasoning. It is necessary to know that lepers—real or alleged—for the most part exercised the occupation of rope maker. By virtue of the fact that they lived outside inhabited areas, they had a large expanse at their disposal for weaving hemp fibers and making their ropes. The folklore expert Claude Gaignebet, one of the best contemporary authorities on popular traditions in France, rightfully recalls that quite often the Carnival fire is called "a border fire," or a *bordelinière, cabanou,* or *cabanelle* fire. These are names for a cabin, to be precise, one of those cabins built in restricted zones: the leper's hut."[42]

Another folklore specialist, Arnold Van Gennep, asked why the bonfires of Carnival were called "cabins" when the property of a cabin—a word that derives, like *cave*, from the Latin *cava*, "hollow" —is to be empty within, something that is obviously not a feature of a bonfire.

This is a question that can certainly be raised, but it shows ignorance of the Celtic style of bonfire. We have a fairly explicit description of one of these in the Irish story "The Siege of Druim Damghaire." During the course of a magical battle the druid Mog-Ruith asked his assistant to build a fire. The assistant "formed it like a churn, with three sides and three corners, but seven doors, so there would only be three doors in the fire of the north.* It was neither laid out nor arranged, but the wood had been piled in heaps."[43] The overall ritual does not appear entirely clear, but it seems that the construction of the bonfire depended on orientation, and that this orientation was based on only three cardinal points. We can therefore assume that this bonfire was not completely filled in.

The hut of the leper–rope maker provides the solution, according to Claude Gaignebet: "The bonfire was originally constructed in the form of a cabin, with scrap pieces of hemp, and built over a hole dug in the ground. Such underground sites are fairly common. Most often they are bottle-shaped. A bench on the bottom allowed one to sit down. Once the lepers or members of the initiatory brotherhoods of Carnival had descended into these holes, the fire would be lit above them. The fumes of the hemp to which they were subjected would allow them to travel into the beyond."[44] European hemp, without having the power of Indian hemp, the famous cannabis, does have the power to induce dreams and has been long used in the countryside for that purpose. It is probable that druids made similar use of certain hallucinogenic mushrooms.

This opens a new perspective on the "human sacrifices" for which the Gauls have been so strongly reproached, and especially calls for an entirely new view of the "burning mannequins." It is a question of

---

*Mog-Ruith entered into this druidic combat on behalf of the Irish of the south against the Irish of the north, who also had a druid building a magical fire for them, but his powers were much more limited.

an initiatory death, thus a symbolic sacrifice by which one may acquire an inner vision of the Other World. All of this falls well within the scope of Samhain, a holiday in which the participants unhook themselves from reality and are able to attain the invisible.

Consequently, it is fitting to consider the tragic death of the king, as described in the epic tales, as a symbolic sacrifice in which the king dies *so as to be reborn a better human being.* As Samhain is at the juncture of not only two seasons but also two years, and the very name of the holiday means "weakening of the summer," the king, who is the pivot of Celtic society, is himself in an entirely weakened state. This is where we can speak of the wear and tear of power. This power needs to be regenerated. The old king must be killed so that he may be reborn. Once this rebirth has been achieved, and thanks to the intimate contact he has had with the Other World, the king has recovered his strength and is able to face the New Year. This is the most probable meaning of the Samhain rituals: the bull sacrifice, the mistletoe harvesting, the symbolic death of the king, as well as the interminable feasting during which satiety and drunkenness allow one to attain a level of consciousness that no longer has anything in common with that of daily life.

two

✚

the fantastic night

a holiday like Samhain that is simultaneously political, judicial, economical, and religious cannot be celebrated in the manner it deserves unless it includes elements belonging to dramaturgy. This has been the case in all societies known throughout history. In Greece, for example, before becoming a series of athletic trials, the Olympics were religious ceremonies honoring Zeus and the gods of Olympus. We could say the same thing about the "circus games" in Rome, which, before becoming an outlet for a populace greedy for sensationalism, were nothing other than ritual sacrifices in honor of this or that deity. From all the testimonies gathered in the Irish manuscripts, it was the same for the Celts: compulsorily, the holiday of Samhain could not take place unless it included "games." What is complicated about the issue, however, is the fact that we do not know just what these games were.

✚ *The Liturgical Games of Samhain*

In all civilizations, including, to the best of our knowledge, those from the most archaic eras, religion and art were generally inseparable. The paintings from Paleolithic caves are perhaps artistic manifestations, but they also contain a religious, or at least a magical, objective. The same is true for all the mysterious petroglyphs adorning the supports of megalithic monuments. These images carved into stone have a purpose that is not merely aesthetic. But these artistic representations come from societies classified as prehistoric and about which, for lack of clear and precise information, we can only present assumptions that are still open to being abandoned or modified. On the other hand, thanks to its writings as well as to its figurative monuments, Greece has left humanity testimony of the first order that can serve as a comparative element if one wishes to study a civilization with an oral tradition like that of the ancient Celts.

If we take the tragedies of Aeschylus as a basis, we find not only the great myths that nurtured the Hellenic tradition but also the incontestable elements of a liturgy that passed from the religious to the profane domain and became in some way a spectacle emptied of its spiritual meaning. However, this meaning remains quite discernible, and the tragedy itself remains a liturgy. The significance of the word *tragedy* is indicative of its sacred origin. Etymologically, it is the "sacrifice of the billy goat," in other words a bloody ritual during which a substitute animal, a "scapegoat," is killed. But in the tragedies of Aeschylus it is human beings—or deities—who are sacrificed in honor of the all-powerful deity who rules over both men and gods without mercy, without compassion—to wit, the *anankê,* "necessity," or in other words, the Romans' *fatum,* "destiny."

All the theater of Aeschylus bears the stamp of this metaphysic so unique to the Greeks, which is incontestable proof that the dramatist transcribed for the use of a secular public only sacred liturgies that even in his era nobody comprehended very well. But the notion of ritual sacrifice persisted within his plays. Prometheus, Oedipus, and Orestes are propitiatory victims, and the ambiguous character of Iphigenia—in *Iphigenia Tauris*—cannot help but bring to mind the bloodthirsty worship paid to the great solar goddess of the Scythians, Artemis, whom the Romans transformed into the "chaste Diana." Archaic elements are not lacking within the work of Aeschylus, which confer upon his tragedies a great authenticity that we do not find in the later works of Euripides. Here everything has become literary, fashionable, and to the taste of Athenian classicism, and thus necessarily transported from the stage of the sacred to the stage of the profane. However, its mythological structure is still quite evident.

Furthermore, within this Greek theater, which emerged from the most ancient sacred liturgies, the audience participated—as elsewhere on a purely epic plane with Homer—in a perpetual confrontation between the visible and the invisible. Humans could easily enter the world of the gods, but the gods ceaselessly projected themselves into the terrestrial world, meddling in the affairs of men and, most often, cruelly and arrogantly manipulating human beings for their own pleasure. All this can be found again in the tragedies of Racine, which, in an ordered and refined form, are no less than the last manifestations of the bloody rituals of ancient Greece. Now, this interpenetrating of the two worlds, the visible and the invisible, this "cohabitation" between gods and men, these interventions of the gods in human affairs and of mortals in divine matters—all are inscribed within the Celtic holiday of Samhain.

But then what are the tragedies that could have been "celebrated" during Samhain? We do not have a one, although this is not to say they did not exist. Outside of several allusions in the Welsh *Mabinogion* and constant references to mournful games in the Irish tales, we know nothing about a hypothetical Celtic theater. Furthermore, the first manifestations that could be classified as dramatic among a Celtophonic people like the Armorican Bretons do not date back any further than the sixteenth century. Again, we should clarify that these were Christian religious dramas that had no relationship to ancient Celtic mythology.

We have a valuable clue here, though. In Armorican Brittany sacred dramas were performed during the sixteenth century. This observation leads to a comparison with the circumstances presiding over the birth of theater in medieval France. We know, in fact, that during religious services, when scriptural texts or lives of the saints were read, there was a tendency not only to declaim them but also to mime certain episodes, with the purpose of making them more comprehensible to an audience of the faithful who were illiterate for the most part, and of firmly engraving them in their memories. As these mimed readings, *an integral part of the liturgy,* grew more complicated and loaded with new elements over the course of the years, the clergy, in the eleventh century, deemed it useful to dissociate them from the worship service itself and present them outside of the sanctuary—thus, in an etymological sense, to render them profane, which means "in front of the temple."

Thus were born *The Game of Adam* and other sacred dramas that, being subsequently embroidered further, became the famous *mistères* (with an *i,* from the Latin *ministerium,* "service," and not the Greek *mustos,* meaning "hidden" or "secret," from which came the French *mystère* and the English *mystery*). As with the Greeks, theater in France had a religious origin, liturgical to be precise. By all evidence, it should have been the same for the Celtic peoples. But where are these Samhain dramas hiding?

The response may be only a hypothesis, but it is quite simple: in the epic and mythological tales in which exceptional adventures as well as the tragic deaths of kings and heroes take place during the time of Samhain. In this respect, three Irish texts are significant: *The Second Battle of Mag Tured,* "The Death of Muirchertach," and the brief but very archaic *Adventures of Nera.* Indeed they appear to be literary tales—intended to be told to an audience—that transpose over a narrative framework older liturgies reduced to the status of oral traditions. These liturgies were no longer celebrated because they were pagan and were transcribed by Christian monks, and they were quite often not understood in their profound essence. These tales bring to mind those scenarios from which dramatists, if they wanted, could have erected dramatic representations lasting as long as a festival, as was the case in medieval France.

The Second Battle of Mag Tured recounts the definitive victory of the ancient gods, the Tuatha de Danann (tribes of the goddess Dana), over the oppressive and dark forces represented by the Fomor. The tribes of Dana had been vanquished and subjugated by the Fomor during the course of a first battle on this plain of Tured, during which their king, Nuada, had lost one of his arms. Now, as the physical integrity of the king went hand in glove with the integrity of the kingdom, Nuada, even with the silver arm he had been given, could no longer claim to rule, and the royalty had been entrusted to a certain Bress, who, through birth, belonged to the two races of the Fomor and the Tuatha. But Bress had proved to be an unjust king, procuring for the Fomor everything they requested, so the Tuatha, desirous of shaking off this odious yoke, had taken Nuada back as king after miraculously or magically "grafting" a human arm onto him. Of course, Bress, stripped of his power, dragged the Fomor into a bitter struggle against the Tuatha.

It is at this point that another divine figure intervenes, one who also belongs to both races: the famous Lugh of the Long Arm, the Master of All the Arts, he who holds all the functions attributed to the deity within himself. But in contrast to Bress, who plays the role of the oppressor, the servant of the dark powers, Lugh presents himself as a hero of light, a liberator. It is thus he who, although not even a member of the tribes of Dana's general staff, leads them to victory in a battle whose countless episodes are so many symbols for the struggle between two antagonistic forces and whose issue is the death of the chief of the Fomor, named Balor, a kind of giant with a death-dealing eye. It is Lugh, himself the grandson of this Balor, who kills this monster with a bullet from his sling, thus delivering the tribes of Dana from their eternal enemies and allowing for a kingdom in full decline to recover its balance.[1]

Now, it is explicitly stated that these events unfolded during the period of Samhain. It was, of course, a mythical battle, comparable to the struggle of the Olympians against the Titans or even, in the Germano-Scandinavian domain, that of the Aesir against the Vanir. One could say that it was a "theogamy" in which the fantastic element highlights the divine functions, in particular that which gives the power of reformation after dismemberment to the gods. Examples are not lacking of gods or heroes (Osiris, Dionysius, and a good many others) who are victims of enemies representing the destructive and dark forces permanently lurking in the universe and who have their body cut into pieces but who are always eventually reborn intact. These fantastic battles are clues permitting us to assume ancient rituals of *regeneration* and *rebirth*.

It is the same in "The Death of Muirchertach," but with a clearly more repressive aspect. As in the tale "The Destruction of Da Derga's Hostel," cited previously in describing the ritual murder of Conare the Great, it is truly because he neglecs his duties as a king and forgets to ensure the harmony of his kingdom that Muirchertach perishes as the victim of the spells of the mysterious Sin. The king has been consumed by power; he must disappear and give way to another, younger, stronger, and more audacious king, as is the case with the Fisher King in the Grail legend.[2] Everything indicates that the events related in this narrative—which unfolds over the time of Samhain, in the midst of phantoms looming up out of the night, on steep cliffs where the noninitiated may slide and find themselves in the abysses of hell—are the essential moments of a sacred tragedy for which the original text has been lost.[3]

The Adventures of Nera, whose text is often obscure because of gaps and archaic elements, is nonetheless revealing of the intention of Irish monks to set down in writing what remained of their ancestors' rituals, even if these rituals appeared somewhat "diabolical." But did they understand their scope? This is not something we can know for sure. In this tale, time has been somehow abolished; all the episodes unfold within a single symbolic instant. King Ailill and Queen Medb of Connaught are in their fortress of Cruachan, in the company of several faithful followers, gathered around a fire where they are cooking some food in a huge cauldron. It is Samhain evening. All at once, the king declares he will give the reward of his choice to the warrior who has the courage to go tie a sprig of willow around the foot of one of the two captives who are hanging in a sort of "house of tortures." The story then enters a strange dimension: "Great were the shadows on that night. Every man wished to go there, but each returned as quickly as they could without having put the sprig of willow around the prisoner's foot. All were scared of the phantoms lurking in the fortress." If we understand this correctly, it is simply and truly a description of what currently goes on during the night of October 31, but with the difference that then it was real ghosts and not children in disguise. The Irish texts make a point of stressing the terror that gripped the warriors, even the most courageous among them.

There is one, though, a certain Nera, who meets the challenge. He is promised the king's own fine sword with a gold hilt if he succeeds this trial. But Nera is a prudent man. Before facing this test, he makes sure to don a solid suit of armor. However, once he arrives at the "house of tortures," his armor falls off three times in a row, and it is one of the captives who provides him the solution for making it stay on: he has to affix it with a nail. This Nera does, and the armor remains on. He then achieves what he had promised to do, and at that moment, the captive says to him: "By your true valor, take me upon your back so that I may go drink with you. I gained such a thirst while I was left hanging here." One will note that the captive was *hanging*, which brings to mind the alleged ritual of Teutas, and that the prisoner was parched, to a certain degree suffocated, which conforms, on the one hand, to what was claimed by Lucan in his scholiast and, on the other hand, to what was depicted on the Gundestrup Cauldron.

Nera acquiesces to the prisoner's demand. He takes him on his back and carries him to the nearest house, and all at once we find ourselves in a phantasmagorical universe. "A river of fire," in fact, encircles the house, and the captive tells Nera, "There is nothing good in that house, because there is no fire without sobriety." They then go to a second house, but a lake surrounds this one. The captive begins speaking again: "Let's not go to that house. They will surely have no tub, not for washing, bathing, or even doing dishes." By all evidence, the prisoner wishes to drink something other than water, and his thirst is symbolic: like all the participants of the Samhain feast, he wants to be drunk in order to unhook into the Other World.

They enter a third house, and here Nera deposits his burden on the ground. "In the room they actually found tubs for bathing and washing, but each of them contained a beverage. . . . After drinking a mouthful from each of the containers, the captive blew the last drop from his lips onto the inhabitants of the house, who all die." Would these drinks be reserved for those who are predestined? We can find no other explanation for making people who exhibited no hostile intentions toward the prisoner or Nera perish in this way. In any case, it is an indication that the contents of these tubs are a sacred beverage. And the sacred can prove to be dangerous as well as beneficial.

Having kept his promise, Nera again takes the prisoner upon his back and seeks to return to the house of tortures. "But he saw an astounding thing: in the place of the fortress, the hill had been burned before him and in the heap of heads impaled on stakes he recognized the heads of Ailill, Medb, and all their followers." We can imagine Nera's bewilderment. And "as a group of warriors were marching into the shadows, he followed them inside the mound." Now the mound, which is to say a megalithic cairn, is supposed to be the dwelling of the people of Faery, the tribes of the goddess Dana. Unaware, Nera, following the bizarre ritual he had been subjected to by his prisoner, has directly entered the Other World. Then everything, time as well as space, shifts.

We realize that the site of Cruachan is on two levels. The upper, apparent level is that of Ailill and Medb's fortress. These two are perhaps mythical beings, but here they are considered as humans, the king and queen of this western province, the poorest in all Ireland, the Connaught. But on the lower level, which is invisible most of the time, the famous sidh is located. This is the domain where the tribes of Dana have taken refuge since their defeat at the hands of the Sons of Milhead (the Gaels). This fairylike—or divine, if you prefer—domain is absolutely parallel to the one above. One finds there fortresses, houses, and fields as well as fabulous riches. So it is in the domain of the sidh where Nera finds himself. He is led before a king, who orders him to go find a woman living alone in a house and to bring him, the king, a piece of firewood each day.

So Nera goes to this house, sleeps with the woman there that night, then performs his daily task for the king. He remains there for an indeterminate period of time, witnessing some surprising things while he is there, such as the presence of a fabulous crown guarded by a blind man and a lame man. He eventually asks his "wife" some questions. She explains that the crown is the magical crown of King Briun that confers supreme and incontestable authority on the person who wears it. Then Nera says to her: "One thing still puzzles me. I want to know what happened that day when I entered the mound. I saw that the fortress of Cruachan had been destroyed and burned down, and that men of your people had killed Ailill and Medb, as well as all their household."

The woman then reveals the truth behind all the phantasmagoria he had witnessed: "That is not exactly what happened. It was an army of shadows that invaded the fortress. But what you saw will come true if you do not warn your people." Nera then asks her how this can be done. The woman answers, "Go back and approach them. They are still around the cauldron, and what it contains still has not been eaten." In short, the woman betrays her own people in favor of Nera. She goes even further, advising Nera to tell Ailill and Medb to come destroy the sidh during the next Samhain holiday. Finally she reveals that she is pregnant and is going to give birth to his son. "When your people come to destroy the mound, send me a message to warn me so that I can find shelter for myself and your flock. As for you, you may return here when you will." But as Nera has doubts that the king and queen of Connaught will find his tale believable, the woman advises him to pick some "primroses, wild garlic, and strawberries," all plants that are out of season during Samhain, in order to prove the truth of what he says.

We now see Nera back at the fortress. Contrary to what he had seen when he entered the mound, he sees nothing abnormal. "It seemed to him that he had been three days in the mound. On arriving within the house, he found Ailill and Medb and their followers around the cauldron." He then recounts how he had achieved what Ailill had asked—to wit, to tie a sprig of willow around the leg of a prisoner. Then he informs the king and queen about what he has learned concerning their destruction of the sidh during the Samhain festival on the following year. Ailill then gives his sword with the gold hilt to Nera and takes steps to mount an expedition against the sidh.

A year passes by. "Three days before Samhain, Ailill warned

Nera that it was time for him to go as previously arranged to protect the woman and her property." Nera therefore returns into the
sidh, where the woman presents his son to him. Then he leaves with
the woman, his son, and the flock, although it is not specified where
they find refuge. Then, "on the eve of Samhain, Ailill and Medb
assembled the men of Connaught and began their assault upon the
mound. After it was destroyed, they carried away all the riches it
concealed. This is how Ailill and Medb gained the crown of Briun
that conferred supremacy over the other peoples of Ireland upon
them. As for Nera, he went back into the mound with his wife, their
son, and their flock, and he has lived there ever since."[4]

A strange story. . . . The dramatic liturgy appears clearly within
the narrative structure. This is purely and simply an initiatory
drama. The first stage is a trial: overcome the fear of ghosts that
haunt the night of Samhain. The second stage, consisting of bringing the "hanged man" to drink an intoxicating and magical beverage, is comparable, for Nera, to Aeneas' possession of the Golden
Bough, indispensable for entry into the Other World. The third
stage is Nera's sojourn in the sidh, where he acquires the supernatural powers of the people of Faery. This lets him ascend to a
level of higher consciousness and acquire something like the gift of
second sight. But he has not lost all connection with his own people, and this is why he returns to warn them of the dangers threatening them. Having done this, he then undertakes a veritable ritual
for regenerating the royal power that Ailill and Medb represent.
Evidence for this is shown by the claiming of the crown of Briun,
as it gives supremacy over all the Irish people. Nera has achieved a
sacred duty: he has been the priest of a strange liturgy that, at the
moment of Samhain, permits the king to regenerate his power,
which is weakening with the end of summer, so that he may confront a new year. Meanwhile, Nera, as a "priest," has attained
immortality and may live outside time and space.

It will be noted that this all took place between two Samhain
nights, which is to say during the length of one full year. The same
holds true in another tale from the Ulster cycle, "The Illness of
Cuchulain." During one Samhain festival, the hero wounds with a

slingshot two white birds that are in reality two young women of the sidh, the fairy Fand and her lady's maid. Fand had fallen in love with Cuchulain, but the wound he inflicts upon her is a kind of insult. Therefore she casts a spell on him that will keep him for a year in a state of lethargy and illness. Going to the Other World during the next Samhain holiday and having an amorous liaison with the fairy will be the only possible cure for him,[5] but he emerges from this adventure more powerful and effective than ever. The claim could be made that in this kind of trial Cuchulain suffered a kind of temporary death, thus renewing his energy and making him capable of accomplishing the most astounding feats over the next year.

✝ The Interconnection with the Other World

What is striking in all these Samhain-related tales is the interpenetrating of the world of the living, the visible world, and the world of the gods, the heroes, and the dead, the world that is invisible but always present, parallel to the world of ordinary life. During the night of Samhain, the borders between life and death are no longer uncrossable barriers, and anyone can pass from one side to the other with no problem, as in that episode from the Welsh tale *Peredur*, in which the white sheep that cross over the estuary become black upon reaching the other shore, and the black sheep become white when crossing over from this opposing shore. This is when what could be called *the passage of souls* takes place. If one thinks on the matter, the carnival-like processions of Halloween are a striking example of this.*

---

*We need to ask what is the real signification of these *danses macabres*, such as those of La Chaise-Dieu (Haute-Loire), of Kermaria-en-Isquit (Côtes d'Armor), and of Kernascléden (Morbihan) in particular. Too much emphasis has been placed on the moralistic aspects of these frescoes with no thought given to the possibility they may be triumphal hymns in honor of the Communion of the Saints, or in other words, the interconnection between the two worlds. Something equivalent can be

An Irish text, *Finn's Childhood*, is quite explicit on this subject. The hero of this story, Finn Mac Cool (the famous Fingal of the Romantics), went to stay with the poet Cethern, son of Fintan, to learn science and divination from him. "He arrived there several days before the festival of Samhain . . . and found an assembly of poets there. . . . Evening fell, and both of them went for a stroll in the meadow beneath a mound that was called the sidh Ele. Finn asked the poet why this mound was called by that name. The other answered: 'Among the inhabitants of this mound is a girl of marvelous beauty who bears the name of Ele. It is in her honor that we call the mound what we do, so much does her beauty surpass that of other women. She can be seen only on the night of Samhain, for during this festival, as you know, all the mounds are open: their inhabitants can visit us and we can visit them, and see their vast domains and walk through their marvelous palaces.'"[6]

As above, so below, declares the hermetic text known by the name of the *Tabula Smaragdina*, the Emerald Tablet. That is the case here. "The sun had barely set when the mounds opened. . . . Finn saw a crowd of people emerging from each mound, exchanging joyful speech. He noted that they brought with them stuff to eat and drink mutually. In appearance everyone seemed to be celebrating, . . . the inhabitants of the mound displayed no hostility toward the people gathered in the meadow."[7]

However, the sacred can be dangerous. Those assembled in the meadow were taking a risk. They were, in fact, men who came every Samhain night to catch a glimpse, be it only for a moment, of the beautiful Ele, with whom they were desperately in love. Each year one of them would be killed mysteriously by a spear. It so happens that Finn had sworn to put an end to this bloody game. He kept watch in the shadows, and at the moment Ele appeared in all her hypnotic beauty, he spotted "a man clad in somber gray who,

---

found in the church of Ennezat (Puy-de-Dôme), which has a painted mural from the fifteenth century that combines three dead and three living people. These visible examples are perfectly sufficient as justifications for the grotesque processions of Halloween.

emerging from the earth, was following the young woman from a certain distance. And this man was carrying a spear." So, at the moment the man raised his arm, ready to cast his spear into one of the suitors, Finn hurled his spear at him and pierced him. "With a great cry of pain, the unknown man collapsed, only to get right back up and flee back toward the sidh Ele, where he vanished."

Finn and his companion Fiacail raced toward the entrance of the mound, but the door was shut. "They then heard great cries of woe arising and from what they could understand of them, the inhabitants of the mound were mourning the death of one of their own, the lover of the beautiful Ele who each year killed one of his beloved's lovers out of jealousy." However, some of the mound's inhabitants who had come out did not have time to get back inside. Finn threw himself in their midst, grabbed a woman by the arm, and dragged her as far away as he could. The woman threatened him with a terrible curse if he did not let her go. Finn did not allow her words to affect him and bargained with her—he would release her only if she got back the spear, which was somewhat magical, that he had used to kill the lover of Ele. "Then, without his understanding how, she disappeared into the mound from which cries and lamentations were still emerging, but soon the door was pushed partially open and the spear of Finn fell out at his feet, still gleaming with blood."[8]

This clearly phantasmagorical adventure is certainly not meant to be taken literally. Finn's ability to kill one of the inhabitants of the sidh, in principle an immortal, indicates quite well that he is enacting a ritual murder of regeneration in which a human being intervenes, playing the role of the sacrificing priest. And Finn's spear, gleaming with blood, thereby acquiring more extensive power, becomes a sacred object. The concept of the annual murder of one of the beautiful Ele's suitors derives from the domain of the bloody sacrifice offered to a deity, in this instance that woman of the mound who, by her beauty, exercises an absolute fascination on those who look at her or, in other words, who worship her.

It will be noted that it is possible to bargain with beings from the Other World when they are displaying a clearly hostile attitude.

Finn himself did not fail to do so. In a later part of the same story, Finn and Fiacail, during what is most likely a Samhain night, found themselves on a hill. They "saw three women mourning on a mound. Intrigued, they approached them, but once they were seen the three women got back up and raced back within the mound. One of them was not fast enough and, catching her by her coat, Finn tore off a broach, which remained in his hand." When she noticed this, the woman came back toward Finn in a rage and ordered him to return the broach. Finn answered her: "I will not return it to you unless you explain to me why all three of you fled." The woman's answer is peremptory: "I do not have to tell you."

The woman started lamenting, saying, "It would be shameful for me to return to the mound without it [the broach]. You wouldn't understand, but it would be an intolerable stain on my honor. My people would banish me and I would be reduced to wandering night after night throughout all of Ireland without ever finding a moment's rest. Give me back that broach, I beg you, and, in exchange, I will give you a gift."* Finn Mac Cool accepted, and once again we see that all's well that ends well.

We see here that it is possible to exchange objects or powers with beings from the Other World. But in this story the possibility of being fated to wander the land is mentioned as punishment for certain banished members of the people of Faery. If we understand this correctly, the banished woman would thus be a ghost. The same idea is found in Christian legends concerning the souls of Purgatory condemned to wander the earth until they have fulfilled their time of penitence or until a living person helps them to accomplish an act of redemption. This is also the theme of the Wandering Jew and Richard Wagner's *Flying Dutchman*. It is thus normal to encounter on Halloween night, beneath the masks and

---

*J. Markale, "Les Triomphes du roi errant," vol. 4 of *La Grande Épopée des Celtes* (Paris: Pygmalion, 1997), p. 72. As the manuscript of *Finn's Childhood* has a gap at this place in the text, we do not know what gift Finn received, but we can assume, based on the other tales from this cycle, that it was the "gift of healing a wounded man by giving him water to drink out of his cupped hands."

the tawdry rags worn under these circumstances, these famous phantoms who have haunted the human imagination for centuries and probably millennia.

Certainly, the stolen broach that Finn returns to the woman from the mound must have had a particular importance: it was probably the emblem of supernatural powers. Shorn of these powers, she therefore could no longer belong to the people of Faery. There is a entirely similar story in another Irish tale, *The Adventures of Art, Son of Conn.* It begins in the Land of Promise, a mysterious country that is obviously the Other World, the sidh where the Tuatha de Danann reside. "The people of the goddess Dana gathered in a great council to debate a matter of the utmost gravity. It was in fact a question of judging a young woman by the name of Becuna Cneisgel* . . . who had contravened the laws and customs governing the people of Faery. The discussions went on for a long time, for no one could agree on a suitable punishment for the guilty party: should she be cast out of the Land of Promise or should she be burned and her ashes dispersed over the sea? Invited to give his advice, Mananann, son of Llyr,† declared that they must not burn her, else there was a risk that the curse provoked by her crime‡ would fall upon the land of Promise and the people of Dana themselves. So it was finally decided that Becuna Cneisgel would be forever expelled and not one of the domains belonging to them could serve her as a refuge."[9]

So here we have one more ghost let loose on the world. The banishment is severe: "Becuna Cneisgel was not only forbidden to find asylum in any sidh of Ireland, but was also banished from the other side of the sea, in Scotland and Great Britain." But here one significant detail is added: "She was sent though to Irish soil in

---

*Becuna "of the white skin," which is the canon of feminine beauty for all the Celts.

†The supreme leader of the Tuatha de Danann after these tribes, cloaked in their gift of invisibility, had to seek refuge in the underground world of the mounds or on the marvelous islands off the coast of Ireland.

‡The story remains absolutely mute about what this crime was.

order to bring her curse there, for since their defeat at the hands of the Sons of Milhead, the people of the goddess Dana hated the Gaels and never missed an opportunity to bring harm to them."[10] This remark speaks volumes about what the ancient Irish thought of these people of the shadows, who were presented as ever ready to intervene in malefic fashion in human affairs. Christianity added to this and made them a people of demons who must be continually conjured away by rites of exorcism. Hence the masquerades of Halloween, which have never been gratuitous.

This is how Becuna Cneisgel landed on an Irish shore, during a time of Samhain, of course. She seduced the king, Conn of the Hundred Battles, who made her his concubine for an entire year. But she brought her "curse" with her, and that year the kingdom became barren. After numerous events that are so many attempts at exorcism, Becuna plays two games of chess with Art, the son of Conn. Becuna loses the first of these matches and must fulfill the terms of an impossible pledge. She succeeds, though, thanks to the complicity of certain members of the people of Faery, because, although banished, she has not lost her supernatural powers. She thus returns to the royal fortress of Tara "in the company of three times fifty young men of the sidh. But nobody sees them, except Becuna, because they possess the gift of invisibility given them by Mananann, son of Llyr."

It is these invisible beings who ensure Becuna's victory in the second match. Art is not duped by these goings-on but can do nothing against them. He too must accomplish a seemingly impossible mission: to bring back a young woman—a member of the people of Faery—without even knowing where she might be. In the course of a fantastic voyage, which lasts for one symbolic year (from Samhain to Samhain), by virtue of his will and courage, but also thanks to the help of certain people of the Land of Promise, Art successfully completes this trial and brings back the *good fairy*, who restores the kingdom's prosperity and forces Becuna, the *bad fairy*, to quit Irish soil and be doomed to wander eternally.

In fact, in this Other World, as it is imagined and described by the Celts, there are as many *good* as *wicked* people, and quite often it is a human being whom the good fairies call to their aid when struggling against the destructive forces threatening the harmony of the "blessed lands." This is the case with Cuchulain, who, to recover his lost health and prowess, must fight on behalf of a king of the Land of Promise. This is also the case with Finn and his companions, who are dragged into the mysterious Land Beneath the Wave by a strange being who arrives in Ireland one Samhain evening riding a monstrous mare.

This tale gives several additional pieces of information about the holiday of Samhain. "Just as his father Cumal and his grandfather Trenmor before him, Finn customarily celebrated the end of summer, during the time of Samhain, with a great hunt in one of the forests of Ireland, then by organizing a great feast in his fortress of Allen. Then the great hall of the dwelling would echo with sparkling conversation, bursts of laughter, heroic songs, and sweet music played by the best harpers and the most skilled flute players of this time. The guests never left the table until they had had their fill not only of food and drink, but also of games and entertainment."[11]

We will note in passing that not only the abundance of food and drunkenness but also the games, which are clearly distinct from *entertainment*, are part of the festivities' program. By way of comparison, it can be recalled that in French medieval theater, the *game* was originally a sacred drama that, becoming gradually longer and more complicated, would be broken by comic episodes, *farces* in the etymological sense, which would soon be separated from the liturgical elements to become complete plays in their own right.

However, it is during the hunt that manifestations from the Other World appear. Finn and the troop of the Fiana find themselves at the edge of the sea when all at once an incredible figure, mounted upon an equally incredible mare, emerges from the water and approaches them. "A person of inordinate size, he had a dark and disagreeable face, the bearing of a savage and ungainly limbs. His left hand, enormous and hairy, held an iron club. A poorly crafted black shield hung over his back and over his completely lopsided left thigh bounced a sharp sword whose blade was much too large. As for his two spears, although of the requisite length, they seemed twisted and bounced pitifully over his shoulder. Furthermore, his clothes were so shredded one would have said he had been buried in them for a dozen years. Finally, the mare he was riding was so thin that the bones of its ribs could be seen."[12]

This description corresponds in almost every point with that of the "churl," a sort of hairy wild man who commonly appears in Celtic tales and the Arthurian romances. Here, he declares his name is Gilla, but from his description and especially because of his club, one could deduce that he represents one of the aspects of Dagda, one of the great gods of Irish mythology, who can be seen again in the very literary character of Gargantua, but whom Rabelais did not invent. This Gilla then demands of the Fiana that he be accepted as one of them, something they readily agree to. But following various events, Gilla drags Finn and some of his warriors on a wild ride on his mare and of course into the sea, until they reach a strange country where the craziest adventures befall them. When they return to Ireland, it is still Samhain night. The Fiana have helped the inhabitants of the Other World overcome their own demons, and in a state where time has been abolished. As for this Gilla, he remains for one year with the Fiana and takes leave of them at the time of Samhain.[13]

This Gilla character thus refers back to Dagda, whose name specifically means "good god" and who is one of the main leaders of the Tuatha de Danann. He is a benefactor, for in exchange for the services rendered by the Fiana in the Land of Promise, he gives them joy and prosperity. It is a little like one of those strange stories in which a queen of the Faery falls in love with a mortal and comes in search of him or attracts him by some spell to her marvelous domain. This realm is most often a heavenly isle, like the one the Irish named Emain Ablach, Isle of the Apple Trees, a strict equivalent to the Avalon of Arthurian legends, an isle governed by women, where fruits were ripe throughout the year, where the vicissitudes of human life are unknown, and where all notion of time is abolished.

The most characteristic and detailed of these stories is certainly "The Voyage of Bran, Son of Febal,"[14] in which a woman of the Faery, in love with the hero, sings a marvelous song to him and gives him the branch of an apple tree, which literally enchants him and forces him to set off on a strange voyage to the land of the Faery. But such an adventure also happens to the son of Finn in the tale entitled "Oisin in the Land of Promise."[15] This is also the case with Condla the Handsome, son of Conn of the Hundred Battles, carried off by a woman of the Faery despite the incantations of his father's druids. Condla did not return.[16] In contrast, Oisin did return to the living, as did Bran, who returned to just within reach of the shores of Ireland—two hundred years later—to recount what had happened to him. In any case, a woman of the Faery does not act against the hero in these stories; instead, she does everything to make him happy and give him immortality.

Accordingly, through these numerous tales, we see that the inhabitants of the Other World, the dead as well as the ancient gods, those who are called the Tribes of the goddess Dana, have the same virtues and the same flaws as the living. They are neither better nor worse; *they simply are*. As with the Greeks, they are subject to destiny, even if they happen to fight and sometimes overcome it. They are not in eternal bliss and can feel great suffering. But they have one obvious superiority: they possess qualities that can be qualified as "magical," and, most important, they know the secrets that humans do not, in particular those concerning the future. And when they know this future, they gladly warn humanity, with the intention of orienting the life of society in a direction more favorable for justice and harmony.

This is what happens in a very short text, *The Prophetic Trance of the Phantom*.[17] This story relates how King Conn of the Hundred Battles found himself—during the time of Samhain—enveloped in a thick fog and ended up in a marvelous palace where the god Lugh unveiled to him his future exploits as well as those of his descendants. The grandson of Conn, King Cormac, experienced a similar adventure, with the addition of an ordeal inflicted by Lugh to test his loyalty.[18] In both these cases, the beings of the Other World are truly helpful in their relations with humans. And all this shows how the Celts imagined the interconnection between the visible and the invisible.

✤ *The Abolition of Time*

Bran, son of Febal, and his companions remained two months in the land of Faery, but they were gripped by nostalgia for Ireland, and they asked permission to take a trip there. They were told never to set foot on the ground. The boat reached the proximity of the shore and Bran engaged in conversation with some fishermen, from whom he learned that two hundred years had passed since they left. One of his companions, being unable to resist, leaped out of the boat. The moment his foot touched the ground, he was reduced to a pile of dust. This was a veritable demonstration of Einstein's theory of relativity, according to which "time depends on the speed of the systems of reference." In this instance, the land of Faery found itself on a planet whose orbit and speed were not the same as those of the earth's. Bran and his companions, within another system of reference, had escaped growing old and thus found themselves immortal, at least as long as they did not leave the realm of Faery that had become their home.

But there are cases where the opposite occurs. Nera, when he dwelt within the sidh of Cruachan, had the notion of a very elongated time, believing he lived there for a number of days. When he returned to the house of Ailill and Medb, however, he found that only a few minutes had elapsed. Here time was lengthened in the Other World but shrunk in some respect in the world of the living. This is what happens on the night of Samhain. There are a good many other stories of this kind in the epic and mythological tales as well as the folktales. The most convincing example of this is the beginning of the very beautiful story *Etaine and the King of Shadows*, without a doubt one of the most curious of the entire Irish mythological cycle.[19]

One Samhain night, the great Dagda, "respected by all because he performed wonders and could unleash storms or calm them, . . . [and because he] protected the harvests and made things so the flocks had rich pastures," came to the feast given by his brother Elcmar in the sidh of Brug-na-Boyne, otherwise known as the megalithic cairn of Newgrange. But he fell madly in love with the wife of Elcmar, the beautiful Boann (the personification of the

Boyne River). She accepted his advances but admitted fearing the jealousy of Elcmar. So Dagda sent his brother to carry a message to another sidh. Elcmar obeyed, but "once he had been gone a little ways, Dagda put some great spells upon him so that he would not return for a year . . . but in such a way he did not feel the passage of time and believed his journey had lasted only a single day and a single night." During this stretch of "elastic" time, Dagda coupled with Boann, and she soon gave birth to a son she wished to name Angus (Oengus), which means "unique choice," and who was nicknamed the Mac Oc, in other words the "young son," because he was the last born of the Dagda. Most important, before the return of Elcmar, Dagda brought his son to another sidh, that of Bri-Leith, to have him reared by a certain Mider, in whom he had total confidence. In this way, Elcmar had not even the shadow of a doubt and returned during this same time of Samhain, convinced that nothing had occurred in his absence of one night and one day.

But this story does not end here. Years later, in the sidh of Bri-Leith, the young Angus is called a bastard by one of his playmates. He demands an explanation from his adoptive father Mider, who reveals that he is the son of the great Dagda. Then, Angus, conscious of the importance of this line of descent, ceaselessly visits Dagda to ask him for a domain. Dagda becomes quite annoyed by this, because all the sidhs of Ireland have a titular head, but he eventually decides that he will entrust him with the sidh of Brug-na-Boyne. His main concern is to expel Elcmar in a way that is completely legal. So he comes up with a strategy that is worthy in every point with the casuistry of the Molinist Jesuits so strongly denounced by Blaise Pascal.*

Accompanied by Mider, he brings his son to Brug-na-Boyne, arriving there on Samhain evening. Elcmar warmly welcomes them. But Dagda takes Angus aside and makes this speech to him: "This

---

*This refers to the theological doctrine of Luis Molina (1536–1600), according to which man receives all the grace he requires at birth; it is up to him to make it effective. —*Trans.*

house is beautiful and I have only seen its like in the Land of Promise. What a fine and pleasant situation here on the banks of the Boyne and the border of five provinces! If I were you, Angus, this dwelling would be mine, and I would cast spells on Elcmar to summon him to leave within the hour and leave me entire possession. We are on the eve of Samhain and you know that during the night of Samhain, time no longer exists. So it would be enough for you to ask Elcmar for sovereignty of the Brug for one night and one day. He is so heated with drink that he will not realize that one day and one night, in the middle of Samhain, is the equivalent of eternity."

Angus follows his father's advice, and Elcmar confers the sovereignty of the Brug on him for one night and one day. "But when this time had elapsed and he came back to demand the restitution of his domain, Angus cast a magic spell on him and commanded him to leave the Brug without delay. On hearing that command, Elcmar arose as swiftly as a bird who has spied a cat ready to pounce upon him."

The magical incantation, a geis, is as constraining as the argument that posits that one night and one day during the period of Samhain is the equivalent of eternity. Human time, which is counted as a succession of days and nights, has no place in a sacred festival that abolishes it by restoring a primitive era similar to that described in Genesis, or even in the Latin legends concerning a Golden Age when reigned the beneficial and protective god Saturn, who was very different from the Greek Chronos, with whom he was subsequently confused.

There is hardly any tradition in which time is reduced to nothing in so radical a fashion. If we accept this reduction to nothing, the process of elimination employed against Elcmar is perfectly legal and cannot be challenged, at least among the peoples of the goddess Dana, within the framework of the sidh, and during that unique occasion during the year of the Samhain holiday. The logic of the Other World, in appearance a world parallel to that of the living, is the same only on its earthlike surface. The metaphysic that upholds this tradition is also quite different. We find ourselves abruptly plunged into a world of gods, heroes, and fairies. But who would they be if not the dead who have attained another world that escapes human laws? The Christian notion of All Saints' Day is not so far removed from this conception of abolished time.

✛ The Profound Meaning of Samhain

The pivotal points of the religious and civil year of the Celts are November 1 and May 1 (or at least from the full moons closest to these two dates). If Samhain marks the decline of summer and the entrance into the "dark months" of winter, the holiday of Beltane is its antithesis. This understanding allows us better to grasp Samhain's profound meaning, which is to say its utility and operation.

At Beltane, the herds are put out to pasture and the stables cleaned, purifying them not only of any physical miasma but also of the potential residues left by malefic entities who would have unduly housed themselves there during the dark months. This emergence from winter is accompanied by merrymaking and also by fires that are lit in the evening before nightfall. This is the festival of light, as indicated by the name Beltane, "fires of Bel," in which the term *bel*, an abbreviation of the Gallic epithet *belenos*, means "brilliant" or "luminous." According to the very distinctive calendar of the Celtic Christians of the British Isles, these fires in honor of Belenos are often confused with the Paschal fire* or have been moved to the solstice and merged with the Fires of Saint John.† Furthermore, the birth of vegetation was celebrated at Beltane and the May Tree (or Anglo-Saxon Maypole) was planted; over the last century this ritual has become the exaltation of the

---

*This is how Saint Patrick lit the first Paschal fire on the hill of Slane several moments before the high king of Ireland lit the druidic fire on the hill of Tara—which was a crime punishable by death, since that authority was reserved for the king—an episode that symbolically marks the victory of Christianity over the ancient druid religion.

†These rituals predate the Celts, dating back as far as the Bronze Age or Neolithic times, when solar worship was widespread throughout western Europe.

good-luck May lily.* And finally, people celebrated the resumption of summer activity with various kinds of festivities and meals copiously watered by alcoholic beverages and filled with various games, the majority being of sacred origin.†

Beltane thus presents itself as the opposite pole of Samhain, but it includes similar elements. From what we know of the great Fiana of Ireland, they spent the summer outdoors, living by hunting and fishing, from Beltane to Samhain. But from Samhain to Beltane, they became sedentary and lived with the inhabitants of all the provinces. This was no more nor less than a period of hibernation during which, like a bear in its cave, they slept, regaining in this way their energy, which had been dissipated by the activities of summer and which was put to sleep during the "black months." Of course, this holiday was the occasion for feasts, which, like Samhain, lasted symbolically for three days and three nights. A lot of drinking went on there, as elsewhere, but the foods, while abundant, did not consist of game or meat. We should not forget that this holiday occurred at the end of winter, and as an old tenth-century quatrain declares: "I

---

*This "worship" of the May lily dates back only to the end of the nineteenth century and was first confined to the Parisian Basin before becoming a quasi-universal custom. It should be noted that in Armorican Brittany, particularly inside Morbihan, even still at the present day, people go into the forest to collect freshly budding boughs of beech to plant in their gardens and fields and to nail on the walls of their houses. When asked why they do this, they respond that they have no idea, but that it is the custom.

†Curiously it is on May 1 that the Festival of Labor was placed, considered during its first appearances to be a revolutionary protest but which is simply a remote souvenir of Beltane. This festival, which has been resurrected as a kind of international folklore festival and completely sundered from its foundations, has spread throughout western Europe—and the entire world—through the intermediary of American unions, directed or animated by Irish emigrants and their descendants. But it is quite obvious that, for want of having been incorporated into the Christian religion, May 1 has lost its sacred connotation and become a political and union-inspired demonstration. It does not prevent the same idea from presiding over it: it is purely and simply a glorification of "work," considered a sacred activity that workers, and generally all laborers, wish to see recognized at its just value.

tell you true, a distinctive feast—these are the riches of Beltane—beer, cabbage, sweet milk—and milk curdled over a fire."[20]

The menu was meager because the herds were providing little milk and less meat. Their health and prosperity had to be restored by sending them out to pasture where they would find fresh and restorative nourishment. We find a trace of these ancient rituals in contemporary Ireland. On the day of May 1, in fact, peasants follow the custom of walking their herds between two fires. No doubt this is to restore the energy they lost over the winter. They also have the habit on this day of lighting a new fire by rubbing two pieces of wood together, which is done to heal any animals that may be sick. This therapy is, of course, accompanied by numerous exorcisms, because malefic powers always stand ready to intervene. So it is necessary to respond.

The Welsh tale of Lludd and Llevelys shows us the people of Britain of that time threatened by a strange scourge: "There was a loud scream that could be heard every May 1 eve over every hearth in the isle of Britain; it pierced the hearts of all the people and caused such terror that men lost their color and strength, women lost the children in their wombs, children lost their reason. Animals, trees, earth, and water all became barren."[21] (We thus see why, with the advent of Christianity, the clergy often went to the stables and performed exorcisms in order to drive out these somewhat diabolical plagues.) After they led a closely conducted inquiry, druids or magicians arrived at the conclusion that this loud scream was being made by a race of small people who lived underground, the people of Corannyeid, whose name is the strict equivalent of the *korrigans* (much like goblins) of Armorican Brittany. But who are these korrigans-Corannyeid of ambiguous temperament, capable of doing the best and the worst, if not the singularly shrunken descendants of the famous Irish Tuatha de Danann, in other words the inhabitants of the Other World who found refuge in the shadowy world of the fairy mounds? The connection that can be made between them is quite obvious.

A connection can be established with a tradition of the Germanic domain—but which must have been Celtic originally, as all the Celtic peoples came from central Europe.* This is the mysterious Walpurgis Night,† which has been made well known by Goethe's *Faust* and the music of Berlioz. This is the night that passes from April 30 to May 1, during which all the witches and demons of Germany gather together in the mountains, particularly the Brocksberg Massif, to celebrate infernal Sabbaths and cast malefic spells intended to render the lands and herds barren. It is obvious that during the Christian era, as well as in earlier eras, exorcism rituals had to be performed to drive off these curses in order to preserve the summer's prosperity, which would in turn allow the dark months of winter to be spent under the best circumstances.

Beltane is thus a kind of inverted image of Samhain, which is not unexpected, as both holidays mark the middle of the year. But while Beltane may be considered to be the festival of "awakening," that of Samhain would be that of "dormancy," during which the secret forces animating gods and men recharge and acquire in some way a new youth. For we should not forget that Samhain is the Celtic New Year, the most important date recognized in the holiday calendar of the pre-Christian Celts.

In light of the observations we have made on this subject, we can thus present the characteristics that sum up the role and impact of this Samhain festival:

---

*The original geographical base of the Celts can be defined as a sort of triangle connecting Bohemia, Austria, and the Harz, places where archaeology has discovered the oldest evidence of their presence.

†Saint Walpurgis (sometimes called Walburg) plays no role at all in this tradition. Born in England at the beginning of the eighth century, she became a nun in her native land. On the strength of her reputation she was sent to Germany by the pope. Saint Boniface, and his brother, Saint Wunibale, entrusted her with the direction of the Heidenheim Monastery he had founded. Walpurgis died after 777. It so happens that toward the middle of the eleventh century, her body was relocated to Eichstaedt's Church of the Holy Cross, which then took the name of Saint Walpurgis. Pilgrimages to her tomb were quite numerous, especially on her feast day, May 1. This shows quite clearly that ancient rituals had been implied in the worship of this perfectly historical Christian saint.

✢ Festival presided over by the king and druids.

✢ Mandatory presence of all members of the social group, all classes included.

✢ A political legislative assembly

✢ Renewal of the king's powers.˙

✢ Judicial assembly (resolution of internal conflicts).

✢ Recording of the collective memory (establishment of the Annals).

✢ Renewal of creation of economic contracts.

✢ Redistribution of community properties.

✢ Feast characterized by excessive eating and drinking to attain sacred drunkenness.

✢ Music, songs, and ritual games (real or substitute sacrifices, new fire).

✢ Symbolic suspension of time.

✢ Intimate contact with the Other World.

Samhain thus concerns a complete festival, during which the religious element permeates all manifestations, even those that appear to be the most profane, because everything paradoxically leads to a vision of the invisible world. In some way, the festival reduces death to the state of nothingness, even if usually there is a separation between the living and the dead. During the time of Samhain, humans see the dead who have temporarily lost their gift of invisibility. We find these beliefs again in the Christian All Saints' Day and the carnival-like rituals of Halloween, although they deviate somewhat from their precursors owing to the slow but steady evolution of spirituality during the early days of the Celtic people's conversion to Christianity.

The Celtic conversion to Christianity was not a revolution but an evolution, during which a sort of fusion took place between druidic speculations and those brought in by the Gospels. Several Irish tales testify to this fusion. This is the case with "The Strange Destiny of the Children of Llyr." Three brothers and their sister are transformed into swans by the curse of their witch stepmother (a classic theme in folktales), and they are condemned to wander this way in cold and privation for three centuries—a length of time

symbolically corresponding to the three nights of Samhain—
before regaining their human shapes. But when they return to their
human form, they have become old, and they die after being bap-
tized by a holy hermit.[22] Now, these "children of Llyr" belong to
the people of the goddess Dana. Thus the tale endeavors to show
the passage from the druidic conception of the Other World to the
new one that is now accepted by Christians overall.

Even more revealing is the strange tale entitled "The Food of
the House of the Two Goblets." The beginning of this story, in fact,
replicates the beginning of *Etaine and the King of Shadows*, as it deals
with Angus taking possession of the mound of Burg-na-Boyne at
the expense of Elcmar. But the details are different. It is no longer
Dagda but Mananann, son of Llyr, who indicates to Angus what
he must do to ensure his grab for power, and most important, there
is no reference to any abolition of time. It is a "charm" or a magic
poem that Angus recites before Elcmar, forcing him to quit the
premises. However, the subsequent part of the story becomes
extremely interesting.

Without going into detail, it can be summarized as follows:
Eithne, the daughter of the Brug's steward, grew up at the same
time as Curcog, the daughter of Angus. One day, during Samhain,
one of Angus's visitors had pronounced some words of maledic-
tion over Eithne because of a very mysterious wrong she had committed. Since that time the young girl could ingest no food, save for
milk, which she had to draw herself from a fairy cow brought back
from the east. "This brown cow is absolutely wonderful, because it
gives milk all year round, and it is an intoxicating milk, to the great
satisfaction of any who drink it." However, Angus is surprised that
the young woman can be nourished by nothing except milk. He
demands explanations from his druids, but none of them, although
aware that it is a consequence of the spell that was cast on her, is
capable of supplying a satisfactory explanation.

It is finally Mananann who finds the answer, which is stated in
a very significant fashion. He has Eithne drink some of the milk
from his own cow, which Angus and he had brought back from the
east at the same time as the brown cow, and he declares: "This

young girl no longer belongs to the people of Angus nor to our people. When Finnbarr affronted her, her guardian demon left her and an angel took its place. She can no longer tolerate our magic. She can drink the milk of the two cows only because they come from a land over which we have no power." The rest of the story will only confirm his opinion.

In fact, one day, probably during the time of Samhain, Eithne and her companions go bathing in the waters of the Boyne. "After frolicking together for a long time, they left the bank to climb back to the mound when suddenly a very dense fog seeped out of the ground, spreading all around and plunging them into almost total darkness. No longer knowing where she was, Eithne called out to her companions, but she received no response. She tried to find her way back through the fog, but the more she looked for the path that climbed the hill, the stronger her sensation became of descending into a bottomless valley. And when all at once the fog dissipated, she was stupefied to see she was walking in a large plain that stretched out to infinity."

By all evidence, Eithne has left the world of the sidh and found herself in that of humanity. She then meets a hermit clad in rough serge who is reading a book while seated in front of a building topped by a little cross. Eithne "approached and, to the man's great satisfaction, began to read out loud the words of the book. Now this book was the New Testament, and the man was a cleric disciple of the Tailgin, the bald man, which is to say the blessed Patrick." Evidently, the young woman remains there for many long months and becomes a Christian, and she recounts in detail all she knows of the people of Dana, "amazing the cleric by her wisdom and intelligence."

This episode illustrates perfectly the continuity that can be seen in the Irish tradition and explains how the Christian monks were able, even when suppressing the parts they considered diabolical and adding to it considerations linked to the new religion, to preciously gather together everything that concerned the pagan era and pass it down in their illuminated manuscripts.

However, Angus cannot console himself over the loss of his

adoptive daughter. He sets off in search of her throughout all of Ireland, and one day he spots her, busy washing linen in the river not far from the hermitage where she lives. "But she did not recognize him, because not gratified with having simply lost the gift of invisibility that Mananann had procured for the tribes of the goddess Dana, she was also no longer capable of seeing those who had been her people." The theme of the loss of certain powers when beings of Faery, through love or some other reason, wish to become human is quite frequent in folktales. This is, in short, what happened to Melusine, who, endowed with mysterious powers but lacking a soul, becomes human, losing some of her prerogatives but acquiring, through this materialization (one is almost tempted to say "incarnation"), an immortal human soul.

But Angus does not despair of returning Eithne to the sidh. He sings a magical song to attract her attention. "She heard the song and raised her head to see where it was coming from. But she saw nothing and could not understand the words that were said. Fearing that it may well be the ruse of some demon, she made the sign of the cross and began to pray. She had not finished her prayer when the blessed Patrick appeared in the clearing. The Tailgin, who understood druid powers perfectly, could see Angus and the troop of the Dana perfectly.* He urged them to abandon their demented beliefs and magical practices to worship the true God." It should be noted that the apostle of Ireland addresses the Tuatha de Danann as if they were actual human beings, and that his intervention here is motivated by his desire not only to protect someone newly converted from the temptations of her past but also to convert all the "pagans," whoever they are, which conforms with what we know of the evangelical activities of Saint Patrick.[23]

---

*According to legend, Patrick, a man of British origin, had been captured by Irish pirates and made a slave of a druid from whom he would have learned a great deal of druidic practices and obtained the gift of "second sight," which would have later permitted him, during his apostleship in Ireland, to undertake "magic combats" against the druids in order to prove that his magic—that of God—was more effective than theirs.

Of course Angus, who understands the Christian's words perfectly, refuses to obey them. But he also grasps the fact that he has lost Eithne, the adoptive daughter who is so dear to him, forever. "Angus and his followers started to run along the river and disappeared with great cries of lamentation. This lamentation Eithne heard. And it provoked such a shock to her heart that she died on the spot. The cleric buried her within the oratory, and since that time it has been called Cill Eithne."*

At present all has toppled. The ancient holiday of Samhain has vanished in the mist. But Samhain survives unconsciously inside this mist to reappear under other guises, that of the popular and fantastic Halloween and that of the liturgical and sacred All Saints' Day.

---

*Cill Eithne means "hermitage," or "church of Eithne." This entire story can be read in Markale, *Les Seigneurs de la brume.*

three

✝

the festival
of all the saints

The Christian liturgical calendar includes four essential holidays that provide the rhythm for the year; this is as true for the Eastern Orthodox churches, the Anglicans, and the Protestants of all denominations as it is for the Catholics who follow the dictates of Rome. In fact, the liturgical year begins at Christmas, the celebration of the Savior's birth; continues at Easter with the commemoration of the Passion and Resurrection of the Redeemer, followed by Pentecost, the symbol of the descent of the Holy Ghost over humanity; and ends at All Saint's Day, the glorification of all those who have reached the Eternal Light. This speaks of the importance of this last holiday, which is, in short, the crowning moment of all successful spiritual experience. But in general opinion, that of the faithful as well as of the nonbelievers, the festival of the saints is linked to the memory of all the dead without exception, because those latter, even if not officially recognized as "saints" by ecclesiastical authorities, can still be considered the Elect.

✝ The Dating of All Saints' Day

Since the earliest days of their history, humans have always taken pains to preserve the memory of the deceased and, in many cases, to make them veritable objects of worship. From the ancient hypogeums of the Middle East to the modern gravestones of the dead that are raised—more or less in good taste—in even the smallest village, there has been a concern for honoring those who are no more and of whom every individual feels to be an heir and continuation. It could even be said that humanity, since its first appearance on the earth, has endeavored to construct an unbroken chain between the living and their remotest ancestors. The care devoted to the construction of these tombs or commemorative monuments shows that this symbolic chain is based on the profound awareness that no human being, although an *individual*, which is to say "singular," is completely isolated from other human beings, whether they number among the living or have rejoined the mysterious regions of the Other World.

But logically, given the fact that a kind of acknowledged or unconscious worship of the dead has always existed in every civilization, one is entitled to claim that there have always been privileged moments permitting contact with the dead. We possess outlines from the so-called historical civilizations with seemingly indubitable traces of these events, but when it comes to prehistory, for lack of written records, we possess no precise indications of a liturgical calendar, including a festival of the dead on a set day within the year. We are, therefore, reduced to conjecture on this point. However, with respect to the megalithic civilization (which spanned the years of 5000–2000 B.C. in the West), it is possible, thanks to recent archaeological discoveries, to date with precision—and with the greatest likelihood—the time of year in which funerary rituals took place.

We know that *dolmens* (a Breton term that means "stone table") and what are called "covered alleys," the inner portions of a cairn, meaning a mound composed of stones and earth, are primarily tombs—both individual and collective. But as is the case for churches built over the tomb of a saint or martyr, these cairns are also sanctuaries. Furthermore, while it is obvious that only several people (priests) could officiate inside a dolmen or covered alley, some of these monuments (in Ireland) offer a veritable circular parvis where a crowd of the faithful could gather. What's important is to know which ceremonies these cairns were used for.

It so happens that during the restoration of the famous Newgrange cairn, the sidh of Brug-na-Boyne from the great Irish legends of the Celtic era, an opening above the doorsill was discovered, and this opening at the time of the winter solstice would allow the rays of the rising sun literally to flood the funerary chamber with light. This funerary chamber, which has a corbel vaulted ceiling, consists of three small apses inside each of which a kind of fountain basin has been hollowed into a block of stone and in which the remains of the dead were housed. There is no doubt that this cairn was the site for rites of symbolic regeneration, rebirth into the Other World, which leads one to think that a particularly important funerary ritual took place at the time of the winter solstice, the darkest time of the year. In consequence of this somewhat fortuitous discovery around 1960, the same phenomenon was then observed in other megalithic monuments, both on the British Isles and on the Continent.[1]

The choice of the date of the winter solstice is not by chance and responds to a kind of awareness held by the people who built the megaliths of belonging entirely to the cosmos and of "vibrating" in tune with its vital rhythm. But other peoples, although possessing this same awareness, did not choose the same date. No doubt this was in obedience to other references that were more in rapport with their geographical position as well as with their intellectual and spiritual speculations.

Accordingly, the Greeks customarily celebrated the memory of the dead on the third day of the festivals they called the Antestherias. This took place in spring, probably because of the symbolism of this season—renewal. The Romans had the holiday of Parentales, which was somehow connected to ancestor worship and fell between February 13 and 20. The ancient Germans preferred to evoke the dead during the period they named the Cycle of Yule, otherwise known as the time of the Christian Christmas season.

Christians have always taken pains to commemorate the dead, considered in their totality as "brothers in Jesus Christ." However, it does not appear that a specific holiday was set aside for the dead during the early years of Christianity, except in the Eastern churches, where it was established in the fourth century as the first Sunday after Pentecost. In the West, it was not until the seventh century that we see the first institutional attempt to set aside a holiday honoring the dead.

It was in fact in 607 that the pope, Boniface IV, dedicated a church in Rome to the Virgin and all the martyrs. But this was not a newly constructed building; quite the contrary, it was the ancient pagan Pantheon of Rome that was thereby recovered and Christianized. In this way the Roman gods of the past gave way to the saints of the triumphant religion, and the sanctuary was given the name Our Lady of the Martyrs. However, no date was specified as to the possible liturgical ceremonies that could have taken place there.

On the other hand, it is possible to fix the official beginnings of All Saints' Day, such as it spread throughout Christendom, in 731. In fact, it was during this year that Pope Gregory III had a chapel dedicated "to all the saints" built inside the church of Saint Peter's of Rome. More important, he made the decision that each November 1 a mass and special service would be celebrated there. This custom was respected from this date forward, but in Rome alone. It was only in 837, under the rule of Charlemagne's son, the emperor Louis the Pious, that it was introduced into Carolingian territory in a general and definitive manner. It was at this point that November 1 became All Saints' Day.

One question arises: Why did the pope of Rome decide that this holiday of the Communion of the Saints would be celebrated on November 1 when the traditional Mediterranean foundation should have directed his selection to an entirely different date, one more in conformance with Roman mentality? The answer is that the date chosen corresponds exactly to that of the Celtic—and therefore druidic—holiday of Samhain.

Irish monks had considerable influence on continental Christianity over the course of the sixth, seventh, and eighth centuries, particularly Saint Colomban, an ardent evangelist and "pilgrim for God's love." He was founder of the famous abbeys of Luxeuil in the Vosges and Bobbio in northern Italy, whose quite numerous disciples spread the so-called "Colombanian" monastic order and liturgical customs that, while often decried by Roman prelates, left their mark upon them nonetheless.[2] Furthermore, during the time of Charlemagne, all the clerics who surrounded the emperor, among whom was the famous Alcuin, a veritable minister of education, had received their religious instruction in insular monasteries that were based on the Irish model. We know today that the notion of Purgatory was a result of the speculations of Irish priests. So we should not be surprised by this concordance between the legitimate papal concerns of valorizing the saints and martyrs and the old traditional Irish stores of knowledge that were transported—whether consciously or not—by the missionaries who came from Ireland and who contributed to the rechristianization of entire regions of the Continent, particularly eastern and northern Gaul, the areas bordering the Rhine, and even northern Italy. There seems to be no doubt that Pope Gregory III followed the counsel of these Irish clerics, who were all highly educated and highly influential, by setting aside November 1 as the festival of all the saints, in tandem with the Celtic tradition of Samhain.

But this Celtic, thus pagan, origin (at least as concerns its dating) confers upon All Saints' Day a singular ambiguity. From what we know of the druids' religion, there was no belief shared by the Celts concerning any kind of punishment or reward in the Other World, no more than there was any distinction made between absolute good and evil. Therefore, every human who died was eligible to move on to another life in one common location. The notions of Paradise and Hell were unknown to the pre-Christian Celts. There was no weighing of souls. There was no judgment but an evolution of the individual to another dimension because, according to the Gallic words reported by Lucan in the *Pharsalia*, "death is only the middle of a long life." The Celtic Other World lacks all differentiation, and everyone has a right to go there.

It is entirely different in Christian theology, which is built in great part upon the Hebrew tradition of the terrible God who punishes the wicked and rewards the just. The holiday of All Saints' Day is thus a glorification of the just, those who "are at the right of the Father." The others are cast out into the shadows, or into the torments of an eternal Hell. The difference appears not only fundamental but also damning in its exclusion. The Christian liturgy of All Saints' Day consists of an exaltation of the Elect through *exultation*. It is a festival of joy and not mourning. It is a festival of eternal life and not a concert of lamentations. The sacerdotal embellishments used in the November 1 ceremonies assert this with the greatest vigor. All the scriptural texts read on this occasion are words of hope, words of plenitude, and words of confidence in an eternal life free from death and suffering and entirely bathed in light, something called beatitude.

But that is all clerical and scholarly theology. If we examine how this joyous holiday is experienced by the faithful, we observe that everything has been perverted. Christians absolutely confuse the festival of the dead with that of the saints, and popular expressions describe unpleasant, rainy weather as "All Saints' Day weather." Meanwhile, the visits to cemeteries and the laying of flowers on gravestones contribute to the creation of an atmosphere of sorrow and anguish that was not originally intended with the institution of this holiday. Everything goes on as if the collective folk memory refused the selection brought about by the official Church and indiscriminately mixed in the Elect with all the dead, whoever they may be. This is obviously a return to the celebration of the night of Samhain, "when all the mounds are open," and when anyone can go from one world to the next in a total fusion of beings from the past, present, and future, a phenomenon that is not in the least paradoxical because during this period time is abolished. This same collective unconscious has preserved and restored very ancient, sometimes now incomprehensible, rituals that currently are manifested in Halloween processions, in which in a symbolic and even theatrical fashion there is no longer any separation between the living and the dead.

✢ The Festival of the Dead

But this persistence of pagan elements within an eminently Christian holiday does not pass by without alarming certain enlightened minds.

Certainly, in every celebration of the mass, the priest takes pains to associate the departed faithful to the Eucharistic sacrifice during the moment of the Memento: "Remember, O Lord, your servant so and so . . ." But this mandatory recollection is made in pursuance of the fraternal community outside of time and is not a supplication to the dead necessarily leading to some sort of ancestor worship. Hence, some theologians have endeavored not to eliminate the pious displays made toward the deceased, but to separate them from the liturgy of All Saints' Day and place them within an entirely different framework. Saint Augustine himself wrote a work, *De cura gerenda pro mortuis* (On the duties toward the dead), recommending the celebration of masses for the rest of the souls of the departed. Many others have emphasized the fact that the living can aid the dead, mainly through prayer. This is how the Day of the Dead first appeared, set immediately after All Saints' Day on November 2.*

The official institution of the Day of the Dead is due essentially to the monks of the Cluny order and most particularly to Saint Odilon of Mercoeur. This individual was born in 962 at Saint-Cirgues, near Lavoûte-Chilhac (Haute-Loire), to a rich and noble family of Auvergne. Having received a brilliant intellectual education in Brionde, where the tomb of Saint Julien was the object of great veneration, he felt drawn by the monastic life, especially following his meeting with Saint Mayeul, the fourth abbot of Cluny. He was made a monk at Cluny and in 994, upon the death of Mayeul, of whom he had become the coadjutor, he was elected the fifth abbot of the famous monastery. He showed himself to be not only a brilliant administrator, founding numerous Clunisian

---

*An equivalent action occurred with respect to Candlemas, assigned to February 2. Once again the influence of Irish monks is incontestable. The Christian Candlemas took the place of the Celtic holiday of Imbolc, the midwinter festival, but as the Irish commemorated Saint Brigitte of Kildare, next highest patron saint of Ireland after Saint Patrick (although this Brigitte is highly suspect, having taken the place of the goddess Brigit, incorporated into the Gallo-Roman Minerva), on February 1, and as there was no question of moving this holiday, it was decided to carry Candlemas over to the following day.

subsidiaries, particularly in his native Lavoûte-Chilhac, but also a great mystic and a man of great charity. Fairly soon, the fate of souls who were not worthy of admission to Heaven had become a subject of concern and even torment for him.

If we are to believe his biographer, Jotsald, himself a monk at Cluny, author of *Vita sancti Odilonis*, which he finished four years after the death of Odilon, the latter made his decision to impose the celebration of the Day of the Dead on November 2 upon the entire order following a visit he received from a more or less visionary pilgrim who had a decided influence on him.*

Here is how Jotsald recounted this odd story. A French monk whose name we do not know had made a pilgrimage to Jerusalem. On his return from the Holy Land, the boat in which he had taken passage ran aground off the coast of Sicily, on a rocky isle where lived a hermit. The hermit and the pilgrim entered into a long dialogue and the hermit asked the other to transmit a message from him to Odilon, abbot of Cluny. Then the hermit expressed himself as follows: "There are places where the souls of sinners, for a predetermined time, are purged of the remains of their sins in a burning fire and with great suffering. The demons who inflict these tortures are quite enraged against those who, with their prayers and alms for the poor, shorten their sojourn in this place and, in some way, make off with the souls they torture. Among these ravishers of souls, the most effective are the monks of Cluny with the Abbot Odilon at their head. So, I implore you in the name of God, if you have the good fortune to find yourself among your brothers, make known to this community all you have heard from my mouth, and invite his monks to multiply their prayers, their vigils, and alms for the rest of the souls plunged in torment, so that there may be more joy in heaven and that the devil may be defeated and spited."

Legend or reality? Nobody knows. The fact remains that on his return to France this anonymous pilgrim made a special trip to

---

*The manuscript of this *Life of Saint Odilon*, which was published by the famous Mabillon, a highly erudite monk of the second half of the twelfth century, is currently housed at the Cluny Library.

Cluny to visit the abbot Odilon and relay the hermit's words. Odilon was deeply moved by what he heard and with no further hesitation immediately ordered all the Clunisian monasteries to consecrate the day following All Saints' Day in memory of the departed faithful, whoever they were, by reciting prayers, celebrating masses, and offering as many alms as possible to the most miserable of the poor. It is likely that this command was put in writing sometime before November 3, 998, so that it could copied and sent to all the establishments that belonged to the Cluny Order.

Still according to his biographer, Odilon de Mercoeur was not content with merely ordering the celebration of the Day of the Dead on November 2, and he took pains to organize the liturgy of this commemoration. "On the evening of All Saints' Day, after the vespers of this holiday, all the bells will be rung and the Service of the Dead recited. On the next day, after Matins, mass will be celebrated for the deceased as on the days of solemnity, to the ringing of all the bells. All the brothers will celebrate the mass in private or in public for the repose of all the deceased faithful and a meal will be given to a dozen of the poor. We wish, request, and command that the present decree be observed in perpetuity, in this monastery of Cluny, as well as in all the other monasteries that depend upon it, and if someone takes our practice as example, may he be crowned by every benediction."

This command, originally reserved for the Clunisian monks, became after 1050 a general rule observed by all the Christian churches. It became an uncontested institutional holiday and now punctuates the liturgical year in the same way as the other holidays. It should be noted that no pope officially declared the Day of the Dead to be a compulsory holiday, but that this custom is presently observed by all Christians, as is testified by the solemn commemoration of Odilon de Mercoeur's decree by Pope John Paul II on November 2, 1998.

This is the way in which the properly spiritual obligations of the Roman Catholic Church were reconciled with the popular traditions inherited from the most remote eras of paganism. All Saints' Day, dedicated to the exaltation of the saints and the blessed, was no longer the Day of the Dead, but through the subterfuge of the shifting of a day, the latter was indissolubly linked to the holiday of all the saints. The separation was only liturgical and not doctrinal, as the two beliefs are in no way contradictory. For this reason it is appropriate to consider Halloween not as an isolated pagan phenomenon but as the indispensable popular complement to the celebration of All Saints' Day and the commemoration of the dead. What is remarkable is that these celebrations are all descended from the same rootstock: the Celtic holiday of Samhain, whose meaning and profundity surpass by far any ethnic, cultural, or even religious cleavage, insofar as this dual notion of the interconnection between the two worlds and the abolition of time escapes any attempt of dogmatic sectarianism.

✣ *Purgatory*

But how does one explain how these once incarnate beings are able to invade the world of the living under a visible form, and on certain nights of the year that are specifically consecrated to them? How does one explain that the dead, tormented in the Other World, could be saved by human intervention? How does one explain, within a rigid framework such as that of Christianity, the possibility of communication between the two worlds and especially the possibility of reciprocal interventions? Folktales from the oral tradition have a wealth of stories in which the dead, unhappy and victims of atrocious suffering, are soothed and finally saved by the intervention of a human being. Quite often, these dead who have been delivered to a blessed state display their gratitude by helping those who saved them during difficult or tragic times.[3] Here again, Irish monks and residents of the isle of Britain have provided answers, and these answers had a profound influence upon continental Christianity.

Among pre-Christian Celts, the notion of sin as formulated in the Hebrew Bible is unknown. In fact, sin does not consist of an act of *disobedience* against a repressive divine law but is the *non-realization* of the individual, a conception that is perfectly compatible with the evangelical parable of the ten talents. Consequently "ghosts" and other "nocturnal beings" who spread out among the living at the time of All Saints' Day (or Samhain, or Halloween) are not necessarily sinners, in the normal sense of the word, but souls who are suffering because they have not, for one reason or another, achieved the role they were intended during their lifetime. In this Other World, these souls demand the right to attempt a new experience, to redeem in some way their past weaknesses either through personal trials or with the help of the living. This is how the very important notion of Purgatory, the place where souls purified themselves before being admitted into the eternal light, appeared in Roman Catholicism.

But the Christian Purgatory is not the Hebrew Gehenna, a place of no differentiation, which, like the underground realm of the Greek Hades, more resembled a garbage dump for shades of no earthly use than a compensatory Other World. It is essentially a stage, a place of purification, according to the standards of the Roman church, where the venial sins that were not serious were expiated, or in other words, where the "mortal sins" are forgiven but demand payment by a veritable "fine of compensation" with a base of physical or moral suffering. The idea of punishment upholds Purgatory, but it is not certain that this notion of Purgatory—for which all historians and theologians are in agreement as to its Celtic, primarily Irish origin—has included from its beginnings components one would be tempted to classify as "masochistic." The Imitation of Jesus Christ does not necessarily pass through the crucifixion of each of the faithful.

If one refers back to all the speculations of the pre-Christian Celts, therefore those who saw in Samhain the "universal fraternity of beings and things," death is a *metamorphosis*, the moment one passes from a state of embodied consciousness to a state of disembodied consciousness. Has no one ever stopped to think that the word *purgatory* comes from the Greek *puros*, meaning "fire," from which the French word *pur* and the English *pure* have their origins? Now, according to the ternary thinking of the Celts, for whom there were only three elements (Water, Earth, and Air), these elements are transformed by what is currently called the fourth element: Fire, which does not exist on its own but is the indispensable agent through which divine creative energy manifests itself. From this we may deduce that Purgatory, before becoming a place of redemption for problematic sins, was a place of transformation.

In fact—and all texts of Celtic origin demonstrate this—the *salvation* of the individual is the consequence of his accomplishment. Genesis states that Jehovah "created man [Adam] in his own image," that is to say, "male and female," and he gave him freedom. Hence the incident of the Tree of Knowledge. But what is forgotten too often is that while God the creator created man (a practical term synonymous for human being) in his own image, he also gave him the power of *creation*, charging him at the same time with the pursuance of the creation that he had brought about earlier. This is why "God rested on the seventh day." He left to humanity the job of continuing this creation. Religious thought has concluded from this that the human being should rest on the seventh day to honor his creator, which is not only an aberration but also a challenge to common sense, an authentic blasphemy against God.

It seems the Celts understood this. For them, according to all their speculations, it is necessary to live to the very extent of one's potential, at the cost of possibly superhuman efforts. This is because one must pursue the divine creation; this explains the heroism of a warrior in the pagan epics who is capable of the most fantastic exploits (for example, fighting four armies by himself!) as well as that of a Christian monk undertaking an uncommon ascetic lifestyle. But those who have not gone to extremes, or who have not dared go there, have betrayed the mission entrusted to them. They cannot enter the kingdom of light. They are the ones who wander in the shadows, no doubt suffering, but ready to accomplish in the Other World what they could not achieve in this one.

Sin is therefore failure. Now every failure can be set right. The Irish monks, those "pilgrims for God's love" who literally infiltrated the Roman church from the sixth to the ninth century, transported this affirmation. While this Roman church has since its historic beginnings always recommended praying for the deceased, the insular contribution had the effect of specifying what manner of prayer would be most effective. It was necessary to save the souls who awaited the time they could enter the kingdom of God. This is the reason that, under the impetus of folk traditions, so many altars consecrated to suffering souls appeared during the Middle Ages.

But this was a non-codified tradition, a kind of tolerance. Belief in Purgatory, which was widespread among the faithful, gave rise to deviations that themselves generated abuses and aberrations. Some members of the clergy, who in truth had few scruples, gladly promised "one hundred days of indulgence" to those who brought them offerings and who performed acts of piety to the letter. In short, they proposed a form of afterlife insurance for the faithful: one could sin in peace by paying in advance for the fault committed. At the time of the Reformation, Luther violently denounced "this traffic in indulgences." It was during the Catholic Counter-Reformation, during the sixth session of the Council of Trent, that the officially codified notion of Purgatory became a dogma of the faith. But this was true only for the Roman Catholics and the Anglicans of the "High Church." Everything remained fairly vague among the Eastern Orthodox churches, and the Protestants of every denomination vehemently refused to put any faith in this notion.

To reach this official recognition, it was necessary to take into account the profound aspirations of the faithful and channel them in order to avoid more abuses in the future. This was achieved by a return to Celtic sources, with the lineage of a Samhain holiday shorn of its pagan elements. The souls in Purgatory continued to wander, but one now knew help for them was possible, and especially which spiritual means offered the best chances of success.

✦ The Protectress of the Anaons

But the image of a cruel and jealous God, the god of the Hebrew Bible, who tolerated no derogation to his commandments, persists in the Judeo-Christian tradition. How does one reconcile this somewhat "puritan" conception of God with another image, one of

compassion and forgiveness? The answer is clear: through an intermediary, an intercessor, in this instance by a feminine vision of the
deity who is both mother, thus a creator and the dispenser of love,
and object of veneration, if not outright worship. This is how the
primordial image of the Universal Mother, the "Great Goddess,"
the "Unnameable Virgin" who is permanently available to all her
children, good and bad alike, who are by nature her lovers, reap-
peared in the collective mentality of the Christianized West. The
myth of Cybele and Attis (which the Greeks turned into the myth
of Aphrodite and Adonis) invaded Christian spirituality and
stepped forward as the solution to all the problems posed by death.

It was obviously the Virgin Mary, the Theotokos officially recognized by the Council of Ephesus in 432 as the "mother of God,"
who would play the role of intermediary between the supreme
power and his imperfect creatures. However, what does this asexual
and merely maternal Theotokos conceal if not the ancient Mother
Goddess of the Middle East, who was specifically honored in
Ephesus, the place where evangelical tradition, furthermore, places
the flight of Mary in the company of Saint John? This ancient
Goddess of Beginnings is also the goddess of the final end days.
She is depicted upon numerous megalithic monuments as a
guardian of the dead, under the form that is sometimes called "the
escutcheon-shaped idol," or even under the stylized form of an owl
head, with a piercing gaze that can keep watch in the darkness over
the deceased. This could only be a female deity who had the ability
to take care of the dead.

In fact, if we go back to the cairn of Newgrange that is penetrated by the rising sun of the winter solstice to restore life to the
dead who are housed there, we are led to make some curious
observations. The architectural structure of a megalithic mound,
for Newgrange as well as for others of the same kind, indubitably
evokes the shape of a woman's belly. It has a very narrow entrance
and an equally narrow corridor that gradually climbs above
ground level before ending in a sometimes quite spacious funeral
chamber—which is never in the middle of the cairn. This is not
even a symbol but a perfectly clear representation of the vulva, the

vaginal canal, and the womb where the metamorphoses between apparent death and real life take place. Also, engravings that incontestably depict a female deity can be found on the supports of numerous cairns.

But take note! Like Russian nesting dolls, one image conceals another, and so on. In most cases the church altar consecrated to the souls in Purgatory is under the patronage of the Virgin Mary. What lies behind the image of the Theotokos officially recognized by the Roman Catholic Church? In western Europe, which was profoundly influenced by the Celts, it is a certain goddess Anna or Dana that stands out in the darkness of the mounds. Here we find in full all the traditions of Samhain, the time when the sidh are open. And who dwells in the sidh if not the Tuatha de Danann, the people of the goddess Dana? Now Dana certainly appears to be the universal mother of gods and men (like Cybele), and it is incontestable that she reappears in the personage of "Saint" Anne, mother of the Virgin Mary according to Christian tradition, but who has never been cited or named in any canonical text.

This has not prevented the Amorican Bretons from making her their patron saint, and we know that in Brittany the *mam goz,* meaning the grandmother of Jesus, has often taken precedence over the Virgin Mary herself. A memory of ancient times? There is no doubt about it. The properly British tradition, one common to both the British of the island and the Bretons on the continent, even made Saint Anne the ancestress of the lineage of the British kings.[4] In folktales it is claimed that her husband, Joachim, was Breton, which gave rise to numerous versions in which we see Saint Anne ending her days on the Armorican peninsula.

But the remarkable thing about the Armorican Saint Anne tradition is the connection made between her and the dead. In fact, it is said that the departed who return to earth to haunt the ways and byways during the night of October 31 to November 1 are Anaons, meaning "Anne's folk."* The relationship of these Breton Anaons

---

*This is a homonymous and analogical etymological equivalency. In reality, the term Anaon is kin to the Gallic word Annwfn (or Annwyn), which designates the

with the Irish Tuatha de Danann is obvious, and even while this folk etymology is false, it is loaded with significance. The great Universal Mother, the "grandmother," is the Goddess of Beginnings and also that of the Final Days, thus the protector of the dead, who are all her children. It is not by chance that a monument to the dead of World War I was constructed within the sacred precincts of Sainte-Anne-d'Auray (Morbihan). On this monument was listed the names of all the victims coming from Breton parishes (including that of the diocese of Nantes, in the province of Loire-Atlantique) who fell during this "heroic butchery," as Voltaire would have called it, butchery that was perfectly useless, nevertheless.

However, Saint Anne did not completely eclipse the Virgin Mary even in Brittany. We could say that there was a merger between the Virgin and her mother, and that both are two faces of a single reality, to wit the Great Universal Mother. In the parish of Brennlis (Finistère), which overlooks the sinister swamps of Yeunn Ellez, considered in folk tradition to be one of the main doors to Hell, the Virgin keeps watch on this portal to Hell, preventing demons from making off with countless children. Didn't François Villon call her, in his ballade "Pour prier Nostre-Dame" (Prayer to Our Lady), "the empress of the infernal marshes"?

It could be said that all of this was true in the distant past, but that would not be quite correct, as can be shown by the following example. What happened toward the end of the nineteenth century in Montligeon, a little village of the Perche (the district of the Orne), proves that the tradition of Samhain persisted despite the Christian coloration it had been given and even through the folklike illusions of Halloween.

On the western slope of the Réno Forest, in the territory of what is currently the township of La Chapelle-Montligeon, stands an enormous church built at the beginning of the twentieth

---

Other World, the original abyss. Thus, the Anaon are literally "the folk of the Other World," just like "the people of the goddess Dana" of Irish tradition, who inhabit the megalithic mounds and the marvelous islands and who, during the time of Samhain, mingle with the human crowds.

century in a very pure neo-Gothic style. This church, which has since been officially elevated to the status of basilica, is the seat of an "expiatory work" whose members are committed to praying for the most forsaken souls of Purgatory, the anonymous souls who wander in imprecise locations, the same spots that were described so colorfully in the mythological epics. The foundation of this work and the construction of this basilica are the work of Father Buguet, a local priest of around 1900 who led a very pious and exemplary life. His spiritual journey is neither without interest nor without a connection to the concept of Halloween.

Father Buguet was born in the Perche region, a wooded area between the Beauce and Normandy, properly speaking, a land of a populace that were very traditional minded but who were still open to the innovations of the new century. He came from a very simple, rural background and was quite attached to Christian values, which had strongly influenced him during his childhood. He became a priest, then was named the parson for the parish of Montligeon. Nothing up to this point hinted at the singular destiny awaiting him, one that would lead him to found this work that would later take on a remarkable life, on both the social plane—with the creation of a printing office and public housing—and the purely spiritual and liturgical plane. But then a strange event occurred that altered the course of his life.

He himself left a personal account of his story: "For a long time, I liked to celebrate Sunday mass for the most forsaken soul in Purgatory. . . . In May 1884, a person whom I did not know came to ask me to perform a special mass for her. Her face indicated that she was a woman of around fifty years: she was then clad quite humbly, wearing the normal clothes of a countrywoman; she had an air about her that inspired respect and confidence. Eight days later, during that mass, which I celebrated at her request and according to her instructions at eight o'clock and on the day decided upon, I was surprised to see her below in the church wearing a sky blue dress and with her head covered by a long white veil that went down to her waist. Who was she? I never knew and nobody could provide me any further information on the subject.

She prayed for a long while before the altar of the Holy Virgin. At noon, how and by what exit did she disappear? I do not know, and despite the fact her presence had aroused the attention of the people of the borough who had come through the church that morning to see her, no one could say where she had gone."[5] There is no reason to doubt the sincerity of this testimony. And yet, what an incredible story . . .

This event had witnesses, and all these witnesses were in agreement in regard to not knowing at all where and how the mysterious woman with the white veil had disappeared. Knowing how strong villagers' curiosity becomes when a stranger is spied on their territory, we have good reason to take seriously the real and corporeal existence of this woman. So what could the answer be: a collective hallucination of the manifestation of an entity who sought to appear for a particular period of time in order to draw humanity's attention to the plight of the tormented souls on the paths of Halloween, those souls in pain who are desperately awaiting a gesture of love that will enable them to find the gate to the kingdom of Heaven? Anything is possible.

The fact remains that this basilica dedicated to Our Lady of Montligeon, the Virgin who interceded with her divine son to shorten the sufferings of these lost souls, currently stands on the side of a hill in a land that was originally and deeply Celtic.

Couldn't the grotesque simulation of Halloween be, even if the actors in this comedy are unaware of it, the temporary embodiments of those souls who wander the border between two worlds?

four

✞

the shadows of halloween

No holiday with deep roots in the past exists that has not replaced an older holiday that has been detoured from its original meaning and incorporated into a different sociocultural context, although it may have been preserved in a more or less clandestine manner in a parallel folk culture before reemerging into the light following extremely precise circumstances. This is how the Roman Saturnalias and the symbolic commemoration of the birth of Mithra at the time of the winter solstice were incorporated and *channeled* into the celebration of the Nativity of Jesus, which then became the Christian Christmas. Such is the case with All Saints' Day, which re-creates the druid holiday of Samhain. But the manifestations of Halloween, although they also stem from this same Samhain holiday, are not mixed into the ceremonies of the Christian All Saints' Day. However, they have been maintained over the course of the centuries in a parallel fashion that was limited to only a few countries before reappearing almost everywhere at the dawn of the third millennium.

✞ The Permanency of Halloween

Ernest Renan, in his *Essais de morale et de critique,* declares in regard to the Celtic peoples, with the pride that his appurtenance to these same people confers upon him, that "no other race took Christianity with as much originality. . . . The Church did not believe itself obliged to react harshly against the whims of religious fantasy, it did not interfere with popular instinct and from this freedom emerged the most mythological cult perhaps and perhaps the one most similar to the mysteries of Antiquity that the Annals of Christianity present."

Renan is an enthusiast who sees in the specific features of Celtic Christianity a kind of justification for its estrangement from the Roman church. He is no doubt basically correct in his assertion that the Church "did not interfere," but the term appears highly exaggerated in light of the severity and even verbal violence that Patrick and the first evangelists of Ireland displayed when combating pagan "superstitions." If we are to believe the legend of Saint Patrick, the apostle possessed a thorough understanding of the rituals and beliefs of the druids (which he would have learned during his captivity in Ulster) and endeavored to show that his own magic—inspired by God—was more potent and primarily more efficacious than that of the druids. We certainly should not take literally everything ascribed to the marvelous life of the man the Irish consider to be their first protector, but it is quite certain that the first missionaries not only had to struggle against local customs but very often work with them as well. Generally, when evangelists found it impossible to extirpate a belief deeply rooted in popular memory, it was instead incorporated and given another meaning and another objective more in conformance with the new ideology. It was out of the permanent confrontation between the ancient druidic wisdom and the evangelical message that what has been called Celtic Christianity, for lack of a better term, was born.

By all evidence, at the time of Ireland's conversion to Christianity, firmness and tolerance were practiced conjointly. Analyzing the apostolic work of Saint Patrick, Dom Louis Gougaud, in his *Chrétientés celtiques*, provides a highly appropriate definition of both their limitations: "So long as the rights of the religion were not challenged, he was of a mind to conform to the mores of the country and present a conciliatory front. But believing him

[Patrick] capable of finding accommodation with paganism on the doctrinal level is a singular misreading of his work. Furthermore, we have texts expressly treating with this topic. The *Senchus Mor* tells us that, when he made an alliance with the *fili,* he demanded they renounce all practices that could not be executed without a sacrifice to false gods.* He left them not a single rite in which an offering to the devil was an element. And, according to the *Glossary of Cormac,* he said that any who continued to observe these old rituals would have neither heaven nor earth, because practicing them was tantamount to the renunciation of baptism."[1]

There is nothing more to be said. The ancient rituals of Samhain were eliminated from the Christian holiday of All Saints' Day, and the evangelists of Ireland took great pains to specify which borders were not to be crossed. Only the idea survived—to wit, the communication between the living and the dead, between this world and the Other World. Christian liturgy could not tolerate the smallest masquerade without disowning the spiritual impetus upholding it.

But this rejection of the pagan ritual did not thereby signify its disappearance. This was when severity was followed by tolerance. It is on the very day of All Saints' Day that homage is paid to the Blessed. Why not leave the previous day, and of course the entire previous night, available for the manifestations—inoffensive at worst—whose intent is to invoke the dead and integrate them, be it only through symbolic images, into the great evocation of the saints? This would obviously separate the profane from the sacred, but there was no other means available. It was better to tolerate the

---

*Around the time of the fifth century A.D., the institution of druidry was no longer what it had been. The preeminent position of the ancient druids, formerly "the most learned" (this is the meaning of their name), had been taken over by the *fili,* who were both keepers of the ancient druid wisdom and incontestable religious leaders. The ancient druids themselves had been relegated to the status of village wizards. According to tradition, it was with the fili that the Church would have concluded its alliance, converting them and accepting some of their customs, which it did in order to respect the structures of the Celtic society.

grotesque in a fixed period of time rather than have it loom up right in the middle of a sacred ceremony.

Everyone received what he wanted: the clerics, because nothing would tarnish the purity of the religious holiday; and the people, because they felt a need to perpetuate an ancestral memory in respect of all that gone on before. Each found its own place; it was a solution that avoided conflict. This is the perspective from which we should consider this tolerance of a church, although intransigent in principle, for manifestations it tended to depreciate by classifying them as a necessary letting off of steam, a purification prompted by excess before the phase of the actual communion. In this same manner, the Church has always tolerated the debauchery of Carnival before the long abstinence period of Lent.

This is how, in respect to the agreements—real or legendary— reached by Saint Patrick and the Irish fili, the rituals of Samhain have endured. They were transferred to the night before All Saints' Day and stripped of all sacrificial context that could have rendered them "diabolical," by virtue of "folk" displays that could serve as an introduction—and a means of letting off steam—to the gravity of the perfectly orthodox liturgy of the Christian festival on the following day.

This arrangement is going to take on particular importance in the extent to which, according to the Celtic mentality, all things derive not from a central power—temporal or spiritual—but rather from a clearly expressed will from the bottom, or in other words, from the ancestral memory of the people concerned. The custom of the monastery-bishopric, so foreign to the Roman conception of a hierarchy derived from a single central point and spreading outward in a centrifugal manner, will play a determinative role in this maintenance. For the Celts, power acquires its legitimacy because it comes from the bottom, and not the opposite. This principle is in absolute contradiction with the Mediterranean system that encourages action of the center toward the "other places," but it conforms with the Celtic mentality that favors the climb of power from the lowest to the most high.

There is one more metaphysical justification for this licentiousness of Halloween, during which all values, if not denied, are at least breached and scorned. You do not construct a building on a site where there once was another without first destroying the old foundations to build new ones. This is what happens on the evening of October 31. Samhain, it has been said, is the point at which summer ends, when everything is destroyed and dispersed. But the objective is not up for discussion: it is a question of destroying so as to rebuild better. As the "New Year," Samhain can bring something new only if it was preceded by dissolution, or *chaos*. Chaos is necessary if one wishes to create structure. The end of the year has arrived and it is imperative that it be destroyed before a new one is constructed. In the complex rituals of Carnival, there is good reason that the effigy of His Majesty King Carnival is burned at the end of the holiday.

There is a principle going back to the dawn of time that can be discerned in the traditions of alchemy. It is the famous *solve et coagula,* meaning "dissolve and coagulate," the first phase of the operation that leads to the creation of the Philosopher's Stone. What can better depict this dissolution, this dismemberment, this destruction, this grotesque and ridiculous challenge to the year gone by, than the processions and shadowy rituals of Halloween? In a way, the past year is being buried—while homage is being paid to it—and, by so doing, one is *symbolically* slaying the king, who personifies the past year because he has ruled it, and this very role has weakened him in a singular manner. Thus the established order is rejected and efforts are made to build another, one that is obviously hoped will be much more fertile, with a greater "high performance,"* and finally more in conformance with a divine order that is not always easy to figure out.

But this did not happen just anywhere. It is found only in this Ireland, isolated from the rest of the world and lost in the middle of the Atlantic, off the normal economic, political, and cultural circuits of western Europe. Now, during the sixth century, under

---

*This is the very principle of every "revolution" that includes a series of real or symbolic murders before achieving a new balance and harmony.

the impetus of some zealous figures, pitiless warriors as well as earnest missionaries—such as "Saint" Colomcille,* founder of the Iona Monastery on one of the isles south of the Hebrides—the northern half of Great Britain, inhabited by Britons and Picts, was conquered politically and culturally by the Gaels of Ireland. The latter imposed their name (Scotia, land of the Scots, one of the tribes of Ulster), their language (Gaelic), and their newly Christianized traditions (heritage of Saint Patrick), as well as their pagan mythology (in particular the entire "Ossian" cycle built around the king of the Fiana, Finn Mac Cool, and his son Oisin). Through the events of history these territories became the depository of the Samhain tradition such as it was lived among populations of at times diverse origin but who had all been melted in the mold of Celtic-type societies.

It was thus in medieval Ireland and Scotland that the practices connected to Samhain were maintained, in parallel fashion to the liturgy established by the Christian clergy for the holiday of All Saints' Day, and apparently without any conflict between the populace and the priests charged with the enlightenment of the faithful. More than ever, during this night of October 31 to November 1, the world of the dead was open to the living and vice versa; time was abolished; and ghosts, a convenient term for spiritual entities seeking contact with humans, could temporarily materialize and engage in dialogue with their relatives, friends, and even strangers who had the gift of "second sight."

---

*It is important to specify that Saint Colomcille, sometimes called Saint Colomba in France and by the Anglicans, is a historical figure from the beginning of the sixth century. He was a member of a royal Ulster family who, after numerous adventures, was forced to exile himself to Scotland. It is important not to confuse him with Saint Colomban, a monk of Bangor, another historical figure who lived at the end of the sixth century and the beginning of the seventh, who went as a "pilgrim for god's love" throughout Merovingian Gaul, contributed to the rechristianization of the northern and eastern portions of the kingdom, founded the monastery of Luxeuil, and ended his life in Bobbio, in northern Italy, in another monastery he had established.

✠ *The Diffusion of Halloween*

The popular holiday of Halloween was able to survive in this limited area of Ireland and Scotland and in the northwest of Europe. To tell the truth, it was confined to these regions for a long time before escaping over the course of the nineteenth century and overflowing the world, primarily the world of Anglophone tradition and culture. If there have always been customs specific to All Saints' Day and vestiges of the Celtic Samhain, it was definitely in an English-speaking milieu that the popular holiday of Halloween developed before erupting in territories where no one was expecting it. This is due mainly to the contribution of the Irish.

The triggering event is unquestionably the great famine that ravaged Ireland in the middle of the nineteenth century following a disease that struck the potato crop, an essential staple in the Irish diet of that time. This catastrophe killed a great many people, but it compelled many others to emigrate, often under quite difficult conditions, toward other countries where they hoped to be able to survive. Among the countries toward which the Irish dying of hunger and misery fled, the United States carried the most perfect resemblance to the El Dorado of legends. In western Ireland, mainly on the Dingle Peninsula, it was commonly stated that the next parish was America. This is not a witticism but a geographical reality. Countless Irish invaded America and set down roots there, some, in time, finding themselves quite favorable positions in society.*

People do not always carry away the ancestral sod on the soles of their shoes, but they always carry their culture and its traditions with them. The Irish—but also the Scots—brought with them certain habitual ways and the memory of ancestral holidays that they

---

*The example of the Kennedy family is significant, but it is not the only one. It should be known that former presidents Ronald Reagan (as indicated by his surname, which means "royal" in Gaelic) and Bill Clinton are of Irish origin, not to mention the "McCarthys," the "O'Tooles," the "O'Haras," the "McQueens," the "McDonalds," the "McNamaras," and other common names of the same genre that built and are still building the United States.

were of a mind to hang onto in the middle of a foreign land, as well as to perpetuate and spread around.* It is accordingly that, during the second half of the nineteenth century, at least in certain regions of America where the Irish element was quite large, the holiday of Halloween was honored in tandem with that of All Saints' Day, which was celebrated with the purest kind of Catholic austerity. Like any colorful festival capable of rousing the deepest—and sometimes the most disturbing—shadows of the human unconscious, Halloween was not only tolerated but also officially accepted, even among the most puritanical milieus of an America in search of its mythic roots..

This celebration of Halloween, which posed a number of questions concerning the invisible world and met the concerns of many people who were not necessarily of Celtic stock, spilled over from its original framework of Irish emigrants to spread throughout the neighboring regions, but essentially within an English-speaking milieu. English-speaking Canada was rapidly affected, although we have to wait for the years 1920–1930 before this folklike and cultural invasion infected, through contamination, the French-speaking province of Quebec. The years following the Second World War, with the mixing of peoples it provoked, accentuated this expansion, which has not yet finished.

We can easily reconstruct the broad outlines of this expansion. The departure point is unquestionably Ireland, a land of Gaelic tradition but where the English language has gained ascendancy over the course of the centuries. Among the Irish, Halloween orig-

---

*In an entirely different domain, that of film, how do we explain that it was in the United States that the theme of the "western" was developed—quite often brilliantly? This theme more or less portrayed sedentary "farmers" opposed to the nomadic "livestock raisers," or even two rival groups of livestock raisers disputing the use, if not the outright possession, of pasturage capable of feeding numerous heads of cattle. If we analyze the structures of the classic western, we find in full those of the great Irish epics of the type exemplified by "The Cattle Raid of Cooley," wherein the hero Cuchulain distinguished himself. See J. Markale, *Le Héros aux cent combats*, vol. 3 of *La Grande Épopée des Celtes* (Paris: Pygmalion, 1998)

inally was the belief that during the eve of All Saints' Day the dead (as the mounds are open) are permitted to return to the environment that had been theirs during their lives and to visit their friends and relatives. But, from another angle, these beings abruptly freed from the Other World are a cause of fear to the living. Might not these latter risk being carried off by the spirits and being unable to return? So people avoided going out on the night of Halloween. However, to display their sympathy for the wandering souls, there was a large number who left their doors ajar: the dead were invited to enter, but only as guests whose duty was to respect the inhabitants of the house. Furthermore, to prove to the dead that they were welcome, the fire was carefully tended and food was left on the table. This would allow the "visitors" to warm themselves and find cheer. Behind this ritual clearly appears the solicitude of the living toward those who suffer in the beyond and who must be aided to the extent that is possible. This attitude conforms entirely to the recommendation made by the Catholic Church concerning prayers for the souls in Purgatory.

From Ireland, Halloween was largely implanted into Scotland, also a country of Gaelic tradition and where the English language was predominant. But the spirit in which the rituals manifested themselves here was quite different, no doubt because the Scots are for the most part Presbyterians, thus Calvinists, and much more "rational" than the Irish Catholics. This is why, on the Scottish Halloween evenings of bygone days, it was not the deceased themselves who returned but young people who personified the spirits of the dead by hiding their faces under masks, veils, or a layer of fat and wearing long white robes or grotesque costumes made from straw. Little by little it was the children who picked up the baton in these masquerades, holding in their hands lanterns hollowed out of turnips or beets, whose flickering flame symbolized the unfixed spirit of the dead. These children would also go in search of treats, treats that, of course, represented the offerings made to the deceased.

All these manifestations, which had a tendency to become codified, crossed over the Atlantic during the middle of the nineteenth century subsequent to the massive emigration of the Irish to the New World, but also under the influence of the numerous Scots who settled in Nova Scotia, the former Acadia where the mix between English and French speakers was realized with a rare harmony. The Irish Catholic state of mind, centered on bringing aid to the deceased, was in some way materialized by the grotesque processions emerging from a Scotland that was too puritanical to take seriously the actual presence of ancestors or relatives on the evening of Halloween.

This is the point at which the very symbol of this holiday made its first appearance. I am speaking of the famous jack-o'-lantern, whose image is currently continued in masquerades. This familiar hollowed-out pumpkin carved in the form of a death's head, with a candle lit inside, originally personified a "wanderer," an Irishman who, according to legend, had not found a place in either Heaven or Hell and was condemned to wander the earth eternally.

First spreading over into the Anglophone areas, the jack-o'-lantern dragged behind it joyful bands of blackened and disguised youngsters, running from door to door asking for treats, some apples or hazelnuts—the symbols of knowledge and immortality. On the facades of the houses—or behind the windows—emerged some rather sinister images evoking in a very precise fashion black cats, ghosts, hideous witches, and more or less diabolical and monstrous grimacing faces, carved of course in those hollow pumpkins lit from within by a candle or bought ready-made—out of plastic—the day before in the closest department store or a small gift and novelty shop.

In this way Halloween crossed the Atlantic again, this time in the opposite direction, to the great satisfaction of the children of the European continent who *play the game* and show themselves worthy of their distant ancestors. Because if these masquerades of the evening of October 31 are so successful at present, it is because the American-Celtic model corresponds perfectly to the latent customs of western Europe, customs smothered or censured for a number of centuries but which were only waiting for an invitation to come back to life.

✞ *Beliefs, Rituals, and Spells*

In truth, it is difficult to make out what belongs to the Christian holiday of All Saints' Day and what derives from a properly pagan tradition. Everything is commingled, as if the popular mentality refused as against nature the border between the profane and the sacred, the real and the imaginary, the licit and the illicit, tears and laughter, and, finally, life and death.

It is generally believed in all rural areas that the night of Halloween belongs to the dead. We know—because some people have witnessed it—that the dead emerge from their graves to go pray in the churches. We also know that all the souls, coming from Purgatory and even Hell, fraternally joined together in suffering and misfortune, form processions and parades along the ways and byways in the direction of those places where they once lived in order to demand prayers or offerings from those who survive. There is a Brittany proverb stating that during this night "there are more souls in each house than there are grains of sand on the shores of the sea."

And it is not only in Armorican Brittany, a Celtophone region, where these beliefs may be encountered. The region of the Vosges—once inhabited by the Celts—is rich in traditions of this kind. We find there that the person who goes out on the night before Toussaint (All Saints' Day) cannot put one foot before the other "without walking on the dead as they are ranked so closely together." At times people have seen an iron ball rolling down a sloping path: it is a soul in torment, we are assured. And one adds: "Woe to the passerby who encounters it, if he does not understand its mute appeal, for he will be incapable of returning home without fear and a great deal of hardship, and especially without smelling an atrocious odor of something burning."[2]

It will be noted that these popular beliefs confuse everything—All Saints' Day, the Day of the Dead, and Halloween itself. We find here the atemporality that characterizes the holiday of Samhain, to wit the symbolic three days and three nights during which the notion of duration given limit and rhythm by the succession of light and shadow is abolished. The Catholic

Church has sought basically to purify this celebration of All Saints' Day by striving to eliminate its more alarming elements—even by diabolicizing them and therefore rejecting them as superstitions and demonic deceits—but it hardly succeeded. These troubling elements, operating a synthesis between the different components of Samhain, are naturally found in the beliefs and popular manifestations of every country, sometimes inspiring fear and even terror, but confirming in every detail that Samhain is purely and simply a period favorable for communication between the two worlds.

Still in the Vosges, mountains that are too easily considered to be under a Germanic influence but were in fact a refuge for ancient populaces of Celtic origin, according to Sauvé, on the eve of Toussaint the beds were uncovered and the windows were opened "in order to allow the departed to take back in the houses the places that were once dear to them." In certain areas of an Alsatian bent in these Vosges, people even left a basket filled with hazelnuts near the chimney so the dead could eat them and find some compensation for the miserable state they experienced outside the period of the holiday. People especially abstained from hunting during this time, because the woods were full of wandering souls and it would be bad luck to wound one of them accidentally.

The same abstention can be noted, still in the Vosges but also in Brittany, concerning digging up the earth. The work of the gardener who plunges his spade in the ground—or the farmer who plows—and hollows out a deep hole is obviously reminiscent of the gravedigger. Furthermore, there is a risk of disinterring some old human remains during this kind of digging or tilling, which would be an evil portent unless this discovery on the very night of Halloween was not immediately followed by the sowing of grain, mainly wheat, because "all the saints who will be celebrated on the next day will come to bless the fields." The Christian theme of Mors et Resurrectio is here recalled in a fashion perfectly full of images for the use of a rural populace whose rustic tasks obey imperatives that are quite precise at times but nonetheless always in relation with the cosmic rhythms.

Now, these cosmic rhythms run the risk of being over-whelmed during the time of Halloween, when time sense is abol-ished. It is said in Auvergne that the sunrise on the Day of the Dead appears in the west rather than its customary place in the east. "The gleam that precedes the sunrise appears on the west-ern side."[3] This inversion should be no cause for astonishment as, traditionally, and among all the peoples of antiquity, Celts, Greeks, and Egyptians combined, the kingdom of the dead is always located somewhere in the great ocean that surrounds the earth, precisely there where the sun sets. During the time of Halloween the dead return, so it is perfectly normal that the sun would rise in the west.

Furthermore, not only is time inverted and overthrown, but the weather also indicates the rebellion of the natural elements against destiny. The saying "All Saints' Day weather" is certainly not gratuitous: this is the time of mists, cold humidity, and dense fogs. Storms may be unleashed against the traveler who has lost his way. Snow may cover the earth and increase the likelihood that the pilgrim will wander astray. Danger lurks everywhere. If we are to believe certain obviously unverifiable traditions com-monly held by a number of European peoples, it is thought that during the period of All Saints' Day (thus a duration of three days and three nights) "the Angel Gabriel picks up . . . the foot under which he holds the demon captive and temporarily restores the power to make people suffer to this infernal enemy of humanity."[4] One would expect that it would be the archangel Michael tem-porarily liberating the great Satan, but whatever the case, dark forces are unleashed and are free to spread throughout the world of the living.

Of course sea voyages are more perilous during the Halloween period. On the Normandy littoral it is said that when the prayers for the dead have been insufficient for procuring rest for the souls of the shipwrecked, a tempest forms in the middle of the night and a boat advances with great speed toward the jetty in the harbor. This ship, with its rigging broken, its sails torn, and its mast teeter-ing, is one that had foundered during the past year. It is then moored to the dock, but when the hour of morning has been sounded at the nearest church, a light fog floats in over the waves. When the fog dissipates, the ship and its crew have disappeared. Of course no one risks going aboard this vessel. Furthermore, to set off to sea either on the night of Halloween or on the Day of the Dead is to confront strange dangers. One might encounter a phantom vessel or hideous sirens luring boats to sharp rocks, where they would break up. In Brittany, it is said that a person can see "a corpse in the hollow of every wave."[5] In addition, those who dare set out fishing during that time will see themselves duplicated aboard their very boat. In other words, each of the sailors would have a double who apes all his gestures. And when one hauls in the nets, one definitely risks finding, amid the fish heads, bones and even whole human corpses.[6]

In fact, given the abolition of time and the intercommunicability of the two worlds, the period of Halloween is "inert." Thus it is necessary to abstain from normal tasks, particularly domestic duties. One should never do laundry in a house during Halloween, for that would entail the death of one of the family members over the coming year. Furthermore, washing a sheet at this time is the equivalent of washing one's own shroud. One should not sweep, either, as that risks wounding the wandering souls, who could seek vengeance. All of these beliefs concerning the presence of the dead during the three nights of Halloween-Samhain therefore prepare the conditions for fundamental prohibitions that are impossible to contravene under penalty of malefic fallout upon one and those close to one.

Accordingly, in several provinces on the Continent, one never bakes bread at the time of All Saints' Day. This would bring bad luck to everyone who ate it. However, in Scotland and England, it is customary to prepare soul cakes, which come in the shape of little round breads, which the bakers sell as a token of good luck. They are generally eaten as part of supper on All Saints' Day. During this meal, the diners take it upon themselves to speak of the family dead and to pray for them, but they do not forget to drink large glasses to their health. Leftovers, in Brittany most often buckwheat crepes and curdled milk, are left on the table to be at the disposal of any wandering souls who might come visit the house. Before turning in for the night, people place on the hearth a special log called a *kef ann anaon*, which is reserved especially for the dead. But in Corsica, people are satisfied with simply leaving out a jug filled with water so that the dead can quench their thirst. And in northern Italy, many people will not sleep in their own beds or will leave them unmade so that their "visitors" can get some rest from their long wandering.

Because the dead wander the roads ceaselessly during these days of Halloween, it is not recommended to leave horses in the fields at this time, for the dead could mount them. "On the next day one would find the horses so exhausted that it would be necessary to keep them in the stables for eight days without letting them work."[7] For the same reason it is dangerous to hitch the oxen to a cart during Halloween night, because the dead could then use them for transport to their former dwelling places, which could be a long way off. Most important, cattle should not spend the night in the pastures on Halloween, because the dead could very well milk them completely dry.

Because communication is established between the visible and the invisible, the period of Halloween is propitious for divination, at least for those who have the "gift of second sight," generally people who have been born on that night. To know who will die during the coming year, one need only to go to a church or a cemetery: the dead will then gather around the reliquary (or the ossuary in Brittany) and give to those who wish—and are able—to hear them the list of the future deceased. But there are other ways to obtain what is called in Brittany the "intersigns"—that is, the signs that foretell an event that most of the time is tragic. In Aurillac (Cantal), "during the night of November 2, at the moment midnight sounded, the specters of those inhabitants of the city who would die in the coming year crossed one by one the abbatial porch of Saint Géraud. They walked slowly and in the direction of the cemetery. There the skeletal figure of Death took them by the hand and led them each in turn to the grave where they would be buried."[8] Elsewhere, in Great Britain, it is common knowledge that the silhouettes of the future deceased would appear in the churches after the twelfth stroke of midnight of Halloween.

There are means, however, of warding off this evil fate. In Scotland a man is posted beneath the porch of the church who is supposed to throw a piece of clothing on every silhouette he sees entering the church. Furthermore, people take cheer from lighting a great fire in the square, an obvious remembrance of the Samhain ritual, in order to keep evil spirits away. But the best means is to cast holy water on the apparitions: they will immediately disappear in the fog.

Because while Christianity was not able to extirpate the gods of paganism from the popular memory, it did give them a diabolical coloration. Everything that is not Christian must be a work of the devil. Now the devil, as we all know, thinks only of doing evil, and in the case of Halloween night, he sends his creatures to the earth in order to bring back with them as many souls as possible. Manichaeism is always present, and the struggle between Ahura-Mazda, the god of light, and Ahriman, the god of darkness, is pursued without end by intermediary creatures. This is the time when a person decides which side he is on and not to succumb to the temptations that Satan's envoys never fail to display to humans. One could even consider the horrible masks that appear during this Halloween night as a means of "causing fear" in the diabolical spirits, or at least of showing them that one is part of the same troop. Incantations can be realized in a lot of different ways.

However, even if the ambiguity persists concerning the beings of the Other World, the duty of humans is always to attempt the impossible in order to save them when they are subject to a curse and condemned to wander for eternity. The justification for the rituals of Samhain was the regeneration of individuals and society through contact with the powers of the invisible world. This idea of regeneration persists in Halloween, and under the influence of the Christian concept of charity, it is inverted. Here the living are expected in some way to regenerate the dead.

Numerous folktales from the western European oral tradition emphasize this "mission."* They offer variations in the details, according to time and place, but they all have the same governing outline. In consequence of certain circumstances, and of course at night (and even if this night is not given an exact date, it is understood to be Halloween), a human finds himself in the Other World. In some versions, he is attending mass, and when the offering plate is passed no matter how deep he digs in his pockets he cannot find even the smallest coin. In other versions, he is wandering the streets of a city where merchants have laid out their displays. These merchants offer various objects to him, but when he decides to buy one, he sees that he has no money on him. He is then ignominiously driven off and often cursed by those he had encountered. Then, once back in the world of the living, he learns that if he had given but a single piece of money to the offering plate or had been able to purchase an object, he would have saved a multitude of people. This kind of story, whose Christian coloration is obvious, nonetheless conforms in all points with the very significance of Samhain: on that night there is communication and exchange between the two worlds with reciprocal interaction. On the spiritual Christian plane this leads to the Communion of the Saints, those of the past, those of the present, and those of the future, within the complete abolition of time and space.

You would certainly surprise a lot of the children who, disguised as ghosts, scatter through the streets in joyful bands on the evening of October 31, going from house to house saying "Trick or treat," looking for a piece of candy, or fruit, or a piece of money, if you were to tell them that by acting this way they are contributing to the salvation of souls in perdition. This is, however, the

---

*One will find numerous examples in the essential work of Anatole Le Braz, *La Légende de la Mort en Basse-Bretagne* (Paris: H. Champion, 1928), which has been continually reissued and constitutes a classic in its field. It is limited to the popular traditions of Armorican Brittany, but the stories gathered and selected by Le Braz have universal value. For other tales of the same type, see J. Markale, *Contes de la Mort des pays de France* (Paris: Albin Michel, 1994).

symbolic sense of these carnival-like parades in which joy prevails over sorrow and the sinister aspect of destiny. These children are *playing at being ghosts,* certainly, but no game is entirely innocent. By receiving something in their hands they establish, on a symbolic plane that exceeds their understanding, a fraternal exchange between the visible world and the invisible world. This is why the masquerades of Halloween, far from being sacrilegious manifestations, are in fact sacred ceremonies whose roots go all the way back to the dawn of time.

conclusion:
exorcising death

Just before his death in 1950 the admirable Welsh poet Dylan Thomas, who wrote in the English language, published a collection of astonishing works under the title *Deaths and Entrances*. In this book Thomas abandoned himself to a kind of surrealist-style mode of writing, which allowed him to travel back through time in his unconscious and arrive at a uterine world, where, in rummaging through its remotest nooks and crannies, he discovered what connects life, such as it is experienced on a daily basis, and nonexistence, that of before as well as that of tomorrow—a metaphysical as well as psychological nonexistence, considered to be a door opening onto the infinite. The poet wrote in a highly inaccessible form—and in an even rougher French translation*—and was, and this is not secret, an alcoholic of the worst degree; he had attained a state of sacred intoxication that placed him in permanent contact with two states of consciousness, which allowed him to participate in both the visible and the invisible worlds. For him, and the title of his collections is, in this regard, perfectly eloquent, "death is the middle of a long life" and

---

*I translated and published some of these poems in the review *Cahiers du Sud* in 1954, thus drawing attention to this poet, who before then had been entirely unknown to the French-speaking world.

causes the one undergoing it to emerge in places other than those he is accustomed to frequenting.

It is a way not of "taming death," as Montaigne said, but of exorcising it by establishing a direct line between *before* and *after,* which will display the permanence of life in all its aspects and all its states. This is the appropriate lesson to draw from Samhain and its survivals, whether the Christian All Saints' Day or the folklike manifestations of Halloween.

But any exorcism of this kind sometimes includes many risks. H. Rider Haggard, author of the famous *King Solomon's Mines,* alludes to this in a strange tale whose English title is *She,* but which in French has been transposed to be *She Who Must Be Obeyed.* The hero, Alan Quartermain, while on an expedition of exploration in East Africa, enters a forgotten city ruled by a mysterious woman named Ayesha. This woman falls in love with the hero and pulls out all the stops to seduce him. She reveals to him that she is the reincarnation of one of his previous lovers, from the time of the pharaohs in Egypt, and that she herself has escaped death after acquiring supernatural powers. However, feeling threatened by old age and devoured by her passion, she decides to perform a ritual of rejuvenation by fire. You would think we were right back in the middle of the Samhain festival. But the trial is too demanding: "She who must be obeyed" regains her true age and falls to dust before the horrified eyes of Alan Quartermain. This story cannot help but bring to mind what happened to one of the companions of Bran, son of Febal, in the Irish tale: following a sojourn in the Other World that lasted two hundred years, he too fell into dust upon setting foot on the Irish shore.

Folk tradition often echoes the failures of an attempt to exorcise death. One Armorican Breton oral story collected in the nineteenth century, "Koadalan," recounts the adventures of a young man who is somewhat naïve at the beginning—like Perceval of the Grail legend—but, following some extraordinary adventures, gains possession of some dreadful, somewhat diabolical secrets, if we are to believe the Christianized version. Thanks to these secrets, he leads a sumptuous existence, but once he has reached an advanced age, he wishes to escape death. To do this, he requests that he be killed, dismembered, and then placed in an earthenware vessel to be buried within a pile of manure. During the space of a year, a nursing mother would come every day to spill some of her milk on this pile. This duration is significant, moreover: it is the length of time between two Samhain holidays, as in the Irish tale "The Illness of Cuchulain." Now, one day before the year is up, the nursing mother forgets to come spill her milk and because this maturation—which is both alchemical as well as magical—is thus incomplete, the hero inescapably dies.[1] It needed but so little for this exorcism to have succeeded.

But the exorcism attempt is sometimes crowned with success, even when it is not by his own free will that the hero undergoes the ordeal. Another story from Armorican Brittany, the "Saga de Yann," provides us with a fine example. This tale concerns a young man born in peculiar circumstances—more or less supernatural or magical—thanks to the aid of a magician, who sets off on a series of fantastic adventures with the intention of bringing back to a certain king of Brittany a magical object this king needs to wed a princess who is no less fantastic and no less demanding. When the young man has successfully passed all the trials that have been imposed upon him, the princess demands of the king that he be burned alive at the stake. But the magician, the young man's spiritual father and at the same time his initiator (who is furthermore presented in the shape of a horse!), provides him with a potion, which he spreads over his body, that allows him to emerge from the bonfire not only unscathed, but even more handsome and intelligent than before—in a word, entirely *regenerated*. It is at this point that the demanding princess compels the king of Brittany to undergo the same ordeal. Obviously, the king perishes in the blaze. The princess marries the hero of the adventure, who is transfigured and has moved on to a higher level of consciousness, having crossed through all the stages of initiation and thereby having exorcised death.[2] Here we find ourselves now more than ever between Deaths and Entrances.

This strange story is incontestably one of the folkloric

recollections of the Samhain ritual in which the regeneration of royal power is achieved through a trial by fire, in which the king— the "old" man—dies and is reborn with a more dynamic appearance, bringing with him the whole of the community he governs. It recalls the theme of "the house of iron heated until white hot" as presented in the Irish tale "The Drunkenness of the Ulates" and in the second branch of the Welsh *Mabinogion*. There are quite a few stories of this kind, not only in the tradition of Armorican Brittany, but also in all the marvelous oral legends hawked over the centuries throughout western Europe. Once again we find the *solve et coagula* of the Alchemist's Great Work is the rule: to exorcise death, one must dissolve within it, the better to be reborn in a higher state.

Is it necessary to be "initiated" in order to cross through the stages of this "death and resurrection"? The question can be raised, but it cannot be answered. Certainly, the *Bardo Thodo*, the *Tibetan Book of the Dead*, insists on this slow process of initiation that allows the soul, at the moment it takes flight from the body, to avoid the vexing and terrifying ghosts who persistently strive to throw off balance the newly deceased upon the paths of the Other World. And the *Bardo Thodo* prescribes remedies against the phantoms of all sorts who assail the soul emergent from a physical body and still arrayed in the deceptive powers of the illusion of existing. . . . But here again, Celtic tradition reveals itself to be much more prudent in this regard, going so far as to say that contact with the invisible can be made in a completely natural fashion with no necessity of prior preparation.

The lesson to be learned from the Irish tale *The Adventures of Nera* is that one enters the Other World without knowing it and especially without expecting to. When Nera, having driven off the ghosts who people the night of Samhain, entered on Ailill's order the "house of tortures" to tie a sprig of willow around the ankle of a hanged man, he did not know he was stumbling into another dimension, another time, and another perception of things. It was necessary for the woman of the sidh with whom he lived to unveil the mystery, thus permitting him to establish a bridge between the two worlds, preserve his people from a grim fate, and find a balance and remarkable prosperity for himself.

This concept of "unhooking," obtained naturally with no recourse to any sort of hallucinogenic substance, can be discovered constantly throughout the abundant fictional work of the American author Edgar Rice Burroughs, the famous creator of the no less famous series of books about Tarzan. It is perhaps in the first book of his John Carter of Mars series, though, that the novelist's metaphysical audacity is carried farthest. The hero, the Confederate captain John Carter, is an aging man. One day as he is riding on horseback through some of the most remote regions of Arizona, he is suddenly gripped by fatigue and seeks shelter in the entrance to a cave, where he stretches out, completely exhausted. Night has just fallen. The stars are shining. The planet Mars is glowing red, at the maximum of its luminous power. All at once, the hero feels as if he is leaving his body. He stands up and sees his corpse lying on the ground, and he is then snapped up by the luminous rays emanating from the planet Mars.

It is on this planet that he sets foot, perfectly alive in the middle of a world that at first appears strange to him but with which he familiarizes himself quickly. He experiences astonishing adventures, knows total and absolute love with a certain "Martine" there, and, at the most tragic part of the story, when he has to save all the inhabitants of Mars following the sabotage of the factory that produces breathable air for the planet, he falls unconscious and finds himself back in his aged body at the entrance of the Arizona cavern, his mind burdened with all the memories he has accumulated during his eventful sojourn off Earth. Dream or reality? The author offers no conclusions, but in the second book of this John Carter of Mars series, he shows us his hero entranced at night by the insidious rays of Mars, putting all his vital energy into this contemplation eventually to find himself back on the surface of the red planet for some new adventures.

To cross through the border of two worlds, from either side, while retaining the possibility of return, has been the dream of humanity since the dawn of time. This is what Edgar Rice

Burroughs has placed in evidence. He is a novelist whose work may be labeled "popular," still at a point halfway between science fiction and fantasy, but which is never found in the course list of selected reading for mythological and metaphysical studies. We can find all this again in numerous films from the American cinema, including the B movies that are devoted to the monsters of Halloween. Here, however, only the subject serving as a starting point is tied to the myths that support the Samhain holiday, and the rest is nothing but mercantile exploitation of the terrifying fantasies that assail the human imagination.

Fortunately there are other films, European films in this instance, that restore to Samhain and Halloween their true dimension, and without expressly saying so but simply through subtly suggesting it. The work of the filmmaker André Delvaux, son of the famous and enigmatic symbolist—and eventually surrealist—Belgian painter Paul Delvaux, is one example, particularly his film entitled *Un Soir, un train* [*An evening, a train—Trans.*]. The main theme consists of the internal problems of a couple, a man and woman who deeply love each other but who have certain difficulties in living their love in the everyday world, all of this taking place in an environment that alludes to the linguistic quarrels between the Flemish and the Walloons. The woman has to take a train to meet her family. The husband, a brilliant university professor (magnificently portrayed by Yves Montand), goes to rejoin her in extremis in this train, which makes his wife very happy. At one point the husband leaves the compartment and walks into the corridor. Then, the pounding noise the wheels of the train make on the rails breaks off. The train is still rolling, but without making any noise; then it stops in a particularly desolate spot in the middle of the Flemish countryside. The husband finds himself alone with an old philosopher whom he vaguely knows and a young man. There is no one else around. The three undertake a fantastic march through dunes, swamps, and bogs before finally reaching a silent town where there is not a single sign of life, except for a noisy tavern in which they seek shelter. The atmosphere is strange and even unwholesome here, heightened by the presence of a beautiful but odd waitress with the significant name of Moira.* Finally, everything switches back and the husband finds himself in the midst of noise and commotion, smoke, and the sirens of fire trucks. A nurse is holding him up. He is okay. He is only dazed. He realizes that the train has derailed. He is led to an improvised morgue where he collapses in tears over the body of his wife.

Dream (nightmare, rather) or reality? The filmmaker does not tell us, although it was undoubtably in his thoughts. He merely leaves it up to the spectator to decide what the answer is. But by all evidence, this story takes place during the time of Samhain, when the world of the dead is open to the living and the world of the living is open to the deceased. And the hero of this film, without realizing it, has performed an exorcism; he has gone into the Other World, for a fraction of a second turned into eternity, which is precisely the characteristic of Samhain. And he returned.

But this experience is usually something that happens alone. The hero of Delvaux's film is the only one to come back. His two traveling companions in the Other World have vanished with the fog. As for his wife, she was already dead when the "fracture" between the two worlds was created. Eurydice did not return from Hades either, and only Orpheus, despite his grief, achieved the initiatory voyage.

The passage into the world of Halloween is truly an initiatory journey. One does not return from it an innocent. But making the journey alone does not mean there was no guide, no initiator, someone who prompted the quest and who, sometimes hidden in the shadows, watches over the comings and goings of the neophyte through this labyrinth that is the Other World. This is quite in conformance with the technique of shamanic journeying. Here the apprentice shaman sets off on a long journey toward the center of the labyrinth, but he must cross through stages that often

---

*The name Moira is ambiguous. It is both Greek and Gaelic. In Greek it designates one of the three "Moiras," which is to say one of the three Fates. She personifies destiny. Oddly enough, in the Gaelic language, Moira is one of the names for the Virgin Mary.

are revealed as quite dangerous, and the master shaman is there, sometimes to see him through the ordeal, sometimes to show him that there are other paths available without thereby compelling him to take them.

This is the central theme of a novel by the British author John Cowper Powys titled *Maiden Castle*. Powys was purely British, despite his name, which is that of one of the provinces in Wales, but he styled himself as more Welsh than the Welsh themselves and threw himself headlong into Celtic mythology, even claiming he was the reincarnation of the famous bard Taliesin. In *Maiden Castle*, he introduces a character by the name of Dud No-Man, who, under the influence of a kind of crazy philosopher named Uryen, ceaselessly lurks about the Iron Age Celtic fortress actually named Maiden Castle, in search of who knows what, and who is constantly brushing into beings whose reality is not certain. Everything here has a philosophical and mythological key. Maiden Castle, literally "fortress of young girls," is the famous Castle of the Maidens that plays such an important role in the stages of the Holy Grail quest, and it is also the Emain Ablach of Irish tradition and the equivalent of Avalon, the Isle of the Apple Trees from Arthurian legend. As for the heroes' names, they are quite significant. Dud means "someone" in both Welsh and Breton, whereas *no-man* in English means no one. Dud No-Man is thus *an individual who is not yet a person* and who is seeking to become one through his initiatory errantry in a kind of Other World. He is guided by this Uryen, a name borne also by a character in the Arthur legend but which, under the influence of André Gide, author of a *Voyage d'Uryen*, Powys considered a French play on words meaning "of nothing." If we understand this correctly, the hero is looking for *nothing*, but he risks discovering *everything* in the course of his numerous sojourns in the Land of Faery, in other words the Irish sidh, in the midst of the imprecise shadows of Halloween.

This theme of initiation is still very present in a novel halfway between fantasy and science fiction by Ray Bradbury. In *The Halloween Tree* we see a group of children looking for one of their friends on the night of October 31. But this child is perched up in a magic tree and from there he has a vision of all the children who are happily and cheerfully celebrating Halloween in different parts of the world. This experience of the ritual seems to permeate his being and lets him grasp what the holiday is truly about. He climbs down from his tree as if he himself had achieved the journey into the Other World.

In fact, the grotesque, noisy, and joyful parades of children during Halloween evening, the evocation of monsters from Hell, of witches and wizards hideously adorned in their depravities, all of this is only a materialization—conscious or unconscious—of what transpires in the depths of the soul of every human being. It is in some way like an exorcism, sometimes by laughter and mockery, always by derision, of the tragic nature of human destiny. It is said there is salvation in laughter because it is a manifestation of a willful defense against the unacceptable. It is also said that the grotesque reduces the adversary, in this instance death, to its true dimensions, which is not worth the trouble of measuring as it is so inconsistent and, in short, insignificant.

But exorcism against death can transpire in a totally different atmosphere, that of serenity. The entire novelistic output of Julien Gracq, the inspired writer who appears as an heir to Chateaubriand, the German Romantics, and the surrealists, is a serene meditation on the themes of Samhain and Halloween. In *Le Château d'Argol,* as well as in *Un Beau Ténébreux,* Gracq leads his characters through very unsettled border zones where it is impossible to distinguish the real from the imaginary. In *Le Rivage des Syrtes,* he goes even further, showing in a very visual and even quite sensual manner the anguished but impatient waiting of humans subject to a mad desire to know the forbidden mysteries hidden beyond the marshes (the Syrtes) in some fabulous country that is always inaccessible without the voluntary triggering of an action toward the elsewhere, with all the risks such an attitude can lead to.*

Le Rivage des Syrtes was published in 1951 by José Corti (Paris). The Goncourt Prize was awarded to this work that year, but the author, who had just published an essay demonstrating the inanity of literary prizes, categorically refused to accept it.

It is, however, in a short novella, *Le Roi Cophetua,* inserted within his collection *La Presqu'île,* that Julien Gracq illustrates perfectly, through myth and symbol, the spirit that animates the manifestations of Halloween. The story is quite simple.* During the First World War, the main character leaves Paris to visit one of his best friends, who is mobilized in the army and engaged in the battles then taking place northeast of the capital, but who is on leave and has taken this opportunity to invite him to his manor located somewhere on the border of the Compiègne Forest. His visitor leaves the train and heads toward the manor. Once he gets there he is greeted by a young and disturbing servant girl who tells him his friend is not yet there but should be arriving any time. She prepares a meal for him and takes him to his room. The friend still has not come and the dull roar of the cannons can be heard breaking the silence of the night. The war is present and not far from their location, but in the manor everything is calm, as if time has stopped. A subtle and fairly disturbing exchange then occurs between the servant and the visitor. They make love for almost the entire night. In the morning the friend is still not there. The visitor takes leave of the servant, leaves the manor, and returns to the station. Once there he notices that it is the Day of the Dead.

Everything is said—and not said—in this tale of an admirable sobriety. What was this manor lost on the edge of a forest, under the permanent threat of machines of war that growled from both near and far? Most important, to what world did this enigmatic and disturbing servant belong? Julien Gracq provides no answer, leaving the reader to decide for himself in his own soul and conscience.

By all evidence the hero of the story did not emerge unscathed from this experience he lived through during the night of Samhain, or Halloween if you prefer. He will never again be what

---

*This story has been adapted and transposed to the screen—and considerably lengthened—by André Delvaux in a strange film entitled *Rendez-vous à Bray* (1963). It is not surprising that André Delvaux would have selected this text, which corresponds to most of his favorite themes.

he was before. He has traveled the strange forest borders where Beatrice led Dante, hesitating between Heaven and Hell, and where the visions of the past became confused with those of the future. He has entered the grotto where Nerval* thought he saw the Fairy—or the Saint—who invited him to share in the secrets of the Other World.

Deaths and Entrances, deaths and initiations [the French title for this work by Dylan Thomas is *Morts et Initiations—Trans.*]. Everything is contained within the apparent masquerades of Halloween. The sacred is inseparable from the profane, and popular memory, still rebelling against the dominant ideologies, has preserved within its most intimate depths and restored on certain occasions a state of nature that was so dear to the Utopian thinker Jean-Jacques Rousseau—to wit, outside of time and space, the universal fraternity of beings and things.

---

*Gérard de Nerval, 1808–1855, poet and essayist who penned his autobiographical account of his descent into madness, *Aurélia,* which the author called his *Vita Nuova.—Trans.*

notes

✠ Part One

1. For more on this subject, see J. Markale, *Le Christianisme celtique et ses survivances populaires* (Paris: Imago, 1983), and *Le Périple de Saint Colomban* (Geneva: Éditions Georg, 2000).

2. Caesar, *De Bello Gallico,* vol. 6, p. 13.

3. I have treated this subject at length in *La Femme celte* (Paris: Editions Payot; 1st ed., 1972; 2nd ed., 1989), republished in German as *Die Keltische Fra* (Munich: 1984), and abridged in English as *Women of the Celts* (Rochester, Vt.: Inner Traditions, 1986), as well as in *Le Roi Arthur et la Société celtique* (Paris: Éditions Payot, 1976), revised and expanded in the English edition, *King of the Celts* (Inner Traditions, 1994).

4. See Christian J. Guyonvarc'h and Françoise LeRoux, *Les Fêtes celtiques* (Rennes: Éditions Ouest-France, 1995), pp. 78–80.

5. "The Foundation of the Domain of Tara," translation by Christian Guyonvarc'h, *Textes mythologiques irlandais* (Rennes: Éditions Ouest-France, 1980), p. 157.

6. Two fundamental tales can be read for more on this subject. See J. Markale, *La Grande Epopée des Celtes:* "The Drunkenness of the Ulates" in vol. 2 *(Les Compagnons de la Branche rouge)* (Paris: Pygmalion, 1997), and "The Feat of Bricriu" in vol. 3 *(Le Héros aux cent combats)* (Paris: Pygmalion, 1997).

7. See Markale, *Le Druidisme* (Paris: Payot, 1985); published in Italian as *Il druidismo* (Rome: 1989); published in Spanish as *Los Druidas* (Madrid: 1990); published in German as *Die Druiden* (Munich: Goldmann, 1996); revised and expanded in the English edition *The Druids: Priests of Nature* (Rochester, Vt.: Inner Traditions, 1999).

8. Keating, Geoffrey, *The General History of Ireland* (Dublin: Duffy, 1841).

9. This tale can be read in Markale, *Les Compagnons de la Branche rouge.*

10. Markale, *Le Héros aux cent combats.*

11. Markale, *Les Compagnons de la Branche rouge.*

12. Markale, *Les Triomphes du roi errant.*

13. See Markale, *Les Chevaliers de la Table Ronde,* vol. 2 of the *Cycle du Graal* (Paris: Pygmalion, 1992).

14. J. Loth, *Les Mabinogion,* New ed. (Paris: Fontemoing, 1979).

15. Markale, *Les Seigneurs de la brume,* vol. 5 of *La Grande Epopée des Celtes* (Paris: Pygmalion, 1997), p. 253,

16. This strange story can be read in Markale, *Les Conquérants de l'Ile verte,* vol. 1 of *La Grande Epopée des Celtes* (Paris: Pygmalion, 1997).

17. See H. d'Arbois de Jubainville, "Une Légende irlandaise en Bretagne," in *Revue celtique,* vol. 7, pp. 230–33. See also Christian Guyonvarc'h and Françoise Le Roux, *Les Fêtes celtiques,* p. 56.

18. This tale can be read in Markale, *Les Conquérants de l'Ile verte.*

19. Pliny the Elder, *Natural History,* vol. 16 (Hammondsworth, UK: Penguin, 1991).

20. *Topographia Hibernica,* vol. 3, p. 25.

21. G. Dumézil, *Fêtes romaines d'été et d'automne* (Paris: NRF, 1975), p. 218.

22. Markale, "La Naissance de Coniaré le Grand," in *Les Seigneurs de la brume.*

23. This remarkable tale can be read in "The Destruction of Da Derga's Hostel" in Markale, *Les Seigneurs de la brume.*

24. Markale, "La Mort de Muirchertach," in *Les Seigneurs de la brume,* pp. 260–61.

25. Ibid., p. 96.

26. Titus Livy, *Ab Urbe condita,* vol. 10, p. 26.

27. I have analyzed this theme in great detail in several chapters of my book *The Grail* (Rochester, Vt.: Inner Traditions, 1999).

28. Markale, *Le Héros aux cent combats,* p. 250.

29. J. Loth, *Les Mabinogion,* Book 1, p. 146.

30. Diodorus Siculus, fragment XXII, *Library of History* (Boston: Harvard/Loeb Classical Library, 1933).

31. Lucan, *The Civil War (Pharsalia)* (Boston: Harvard, 1928), p. 451.

32. "Branwen, Daughter of Llyr," in J. Loth, *Les Mabinogion,* p. 129.

33. "Peredur, fils d'Wvrawc," in J. Loth, *Les Mabinogion,* p. 94.

34. *Olympiads,* I, 40.

35. Markale, *La Naissance du roi Arthur,* vol. 1 of the *Cycle du Graal* (Paris: Pygmalion, 1992).

36. See Markale, *Les Conquerants de l'Ile verte.*

37. J. Loth, *Les Mabinogion,* Book 1, p. 335.

38. Ibid., pp. 130–32.

39. Translation, Christian Guyonvarc'h, *Ogam,* vol. 13.

40. Caesar, *De Bello Gallico,* vol. 6, p. 16.

41. Ibid., vol. 5, p. 5.

42. Claude Gaignebet, *Le Carnaval* (Paris: Payot, 1974), p. 74.

43. Translation by M. L. Sjoestedt in *Revue celtique,* vol. 43, p. 109.

44. Gaignebet, *Le Carnaval,* p. 74.

✣ *Part Two*

1. One can read the tale of this battle in Markale, *Les Conquérants de l'Ile verte,* vol. 1 of *La Grande Epopée des Celtes* (Paris: Pygmalion, 1997).

2. See Markale, *Galaad et le Roi Pêcheur,* vol. 7 of the *Cycle du Graal* (Paris: Pygmalion, 1997).

3. This story can be read in Markale, *Les Seigneurs de la brume,* vol. 5 of *La Grande Epopée des Celtes* (Paris: Pygmalion, 1997).

4. The complete story can be found in Markale, "Demons et Merveilles," in *Les Conquérants de l'Ile verte.*

5. This entire story can be found in Markale, *Le Héros aux cent combats,* vol. 3 of *La Grande Épopée des Celtes* (Paris: Éditions Pygmalion, 1997).

6. Markale, *Les Triomphes du roi errant,* vol. 4 of *La Grande Épopée des Celtes* (Paris: Pygmalion, 1997), p. 67.

7. Ibid., p. 71.

8. Ibid.

9. Markale, *Les Seigneurs de la brume,* pp. 115–16.

10. Ibid., p. 116.

11. Markale, *Les Triomphes du roi errant*, p. 112.

12. Ibid., p. 113.

13. The complete story is included in Markale, *Les Triomphes du roi errant*.

14. The complete story is included in Markale, "La Terre des Fées," in *Les Conquérants de l'Ile verte*.

15. The complete story is included in Markale, *Les Triomphes du roi errant*.

16. The complete story is included in Markale, *Les Seigneurs de la brume*.

17. Ibid.

18. Ibid.

19. Markale, "Les Tribulations du jeune Angus," in *Les Conquérants de l'Ile verte*.

20. Kuno Meyer, *Hibernica Minora* (Oxford: Nutt, 1894).

21. J. Loth, *Les Mabinogion* (Paris: Fontemoing, 1979), Book II, p. 234.

22. The complete story can be found in Markale, *Les Conquérants de l'Ile verte*.

23. See Markale, *Le Christianisme celtique et ses survivances populaires* (Paris: Imago, 1983).

✢ Part Three

1. See Markale, *Dolmens et Menhirs: la civilisation mégalithique* (Paris: Payot, 1994).

2. For more on this topic, see Markale, *Le Christianisme celtique et ses*

survivances populaires (Paris: Imago, 1983), as well as *Le Périple de Saint Colomban* (Geneva: Éditions Georg, 2000).

3. The reader can find numerous stories of this sort in Markale, *Contes de la Mort des pays de France* (Paris: Albin Michel, 1994).

4. See the first chapter, titled "The Drowned City or the Celtic Myth of Origin," of Markale, *The Celts: Uncovering the Mythic and Historic Origins of Western Culture* (Rochester, Vt.: Inner Traditions, 1993).

5. Abbé Eugène Labelle, *Petite Histoire de Notre-Dame de Montligeon* (Paris: Édition Tolra, 1935), p. 8.

Part Four

1. W. Stokes, *Three Irish Glossaries* (London: Williams and Norgate, 1862), p. 25.

2. L. Sauvé, *Le Folklore des Vosges,* New ed. (Rosheim: Maisonneuve et Larose, 1984).

3. *Revue des Traditions populaires,* vol. 13, p. 99.

4. A. de Chesnel, *Dictionnaire des superstitions, erreurs, préjugés et traditions populaires où sont exposées les croyances superstitieuses des temps anciens et modernes,* vol. 20 of the *Encyclopédie théologique* (Paris: 1856).

5. *Dictionnaire des superstitions,* Forcalquier: 1967.

6. Ibid.

7. A. Van Gennep, *Manuel de Folklore contemporain* (Paris: Stock, 1935–1958).

8. *Revue des Traditions populaires,* vol. 8, p. 122.

✝ Conclusion

1. The complete story can be found in Markale, *La Tradition celtique en Bretagne armoricaine* (Paris: Payot, 1975). The final part of this story was reprinted in Markale, *Contes de la Mort des pays de France* (Paris: Albin Michel, 1994).

2. The complete story can be found in Markale, *La Tradition celtique en Bretagne armoricaine.*

BIBLIOGRAPHY

Bertrand, Alexandre. *La Religion des Gaulois.* Paris: Ernest Leroux, 1897.

Bradbury, Ray. *The Halloween Tree.* New York: Knopf, 1988.

Brekilien, Yann. *La Mythology celtique.* Paris: Jean Picollec, 1980.

Burroughs, Edgar Rice. *John Carter of Mars.* New York: Canaveral Press, 1964.

Caesar. *De Bello Gallico.* Boston: Harvard/Loeb Classical Library, 1917.

Cambrensis, Geraldus. *Topographia Hibernica,* vol. 3.

de Jubainville, H. d'Arbois. *Le Cycle mythologique irlandais.* Paris: Ernest Thorin, 1884.

——. "Une Légende irlandaise en Bretagne." *Revue celtique,* vol. 7.

Dontenville, Henri. *La Mythologie française.* Paris: Payot,1973.

Dottin, Georges. *La Religion des Celtes.* Paris: Payot, 1904.

——. *L'Epopée irlandaise.* New ed. Paris: Les Cent Chef d'Oeuvres Étrangers, 1980.

Dumézil, Georges. *Fêtes romaines d'été et d'automne.* Paris: NRF, 1975.

Eliade, Mircea. *A History of Religious Ideas: From Muhammed to the Age of Reforms,* vol. 3. Chicago: University of Chicago Press, 1988.

——. *Shamanism.* 2nd ed. Princeton: Princeton/Bollingen, 1972.

Evans-Wentz, W. Y. *The Tibetan Book of the Dead.* London: Oxford, 1949.

Frazer, James. *The New Golden Bough.* New York: Criterion Books, 1959.

Gaignebet, Claude. *Le Carnaval.* Paris: Payot, 1974.

Gracq, Julien. *Le Château d'Argol.* Paris: José Corti, 1938. Translated into English by Louise Varèse as *The Castle of Argol* (New York: New Directions, 1951).

——. *La Presqu'île.* 3rd ed. Paris: José Corti, 1970.

——. *Le Rivage des Syrtes.* Paris: José Corti, 1951. Translated into English by Richard Howard as *The Opposing Shore* (New York: Columbia University Press, 1986).

——. *Un Beau Ténébreux.* Paris: José Corti, 1945. Translated into English by W. J. Strachan as *The Dark Stranger* (New York: New Directions, 1951).

Guyonvarc'h, Christian, trans. *Ogam,* vol. 10.

——. *Ogam,* vol. 13.

Guyonvarc'h, Christian. *Textes mythologiques irlandais.* Rennes: Éditions Ouest-France, 1980.

Guyonvarc'h, Christian and Françoise Le Roux. *Les Druides.* Rennes: Éditions Ouest-France, 1978.

——. *Les Fêtes celtiques.* Rennes: Éditions Ouest-France, 1995.

Haggard, H. Rider. *She.* London: W. L. Allison Co., 1893.

Keating, Geoffrey. *The General History of Ireland.* Dublin: Duffy, 1841.

Labelle, Eugène, Abbé, *Petite Histoire de Notre-Dame de Montligeon.* Paris: Édition Tolra, 1935.

Le Braz, Anatole. *La Légende de la Mort en Basse-Bretagne.* Paris: H. Champion, 1928.

Livy, Titus. *The Early History of Rome.* 5 volumes. Hammondsworth, UK: Penguin, 1973.

Livy, Titus. *Historiarum Ab Urbe condita Libri.* Qui extant. XXXV cum universae historiae epitomia. Venice: Paulus Manitius (Aldus), 1555.

Loth, Joseph. *Les Mabinogion.* New ed. Paris: Fontemoing, 1979.

Loyer, Olivier. *Les Chrétientés celtiques.* Paris: P.U.F., 1965.

Lucan. *The Civil War (Pharsalia).* Boston: Harvard, 1928.

Markale, Jean. *The Celts: Uncovering the Mythic and Historic Origins of Western Culture.* Rochester, Vt.: Inner Traditions, 1993.

——. *Le Christianisme celtique et ses survivances populaires.* Paris: Imago, 1983.

——. *Contes de la Mort des pays de France.* Paris: Albin Michel, 1994.

——. *Contes populaires de toutes les Bretagnes.* Rennes: Éditions Ouest-France, 1977.

——. *Cycle du Graal.* 7 volumes. Paris: Pygmalion, 1992–1997.

——. *Dolmens et Menhirs: la civilisation mégalithique.* Paris: Payot, 1994.

——. *The Druids: Priests of Nature.* Rochester, Vt.: Inner Traditions, 1999.

——. *The Epics of Celtic Ireland: Ancient Tales of Mystery and Magic.* Rochester, Vt.: Inner Traditions, 2000.

——. *The Grail.* Rochester, Vt.: Inner Traditions, 1999.

——. *La Grande Epopée des Celtes.* 5 volumes. Paris: Pygmalion, 1997–1999.

——. *King of the Celts.* Rochester, Vt.: Inner Traditions, 1994.

——. *Nouveau Dictionnaire de mythologie celtique.* Paris: Pygmalion, 1998.

——. *Le Périple de Saint Colomban.* Geneva: Éditions Georg, 2000.

——. *La Tradition celtique en Bretagne armoricaine.* Paris: Payot, 1975.

——. *Women of the Celts.* Rochester, Vt.: Inner Traditions, 1986.

Meyer, Kuno. *Hibernica Minora.* Oxford: Nutt, 1894.

Pliny the Elder. *Natural History,* XVI. Hammondsworth, UK: Penguin, 1991.

Powys, John Cowper. *Maiden Castle.* New York: Simon & Schuster, 1936.

Rabelais, François. *Gargantua and Pantagruel.* Baltimore: Penguin, 1955.

Reinach, Salomon. *Cultes, Mythes et Religions.* 4 volumes. Paris: Ernest Leroux, 1905–1912.

Sauvé, Léopold-François. *Le Folklore des Vosges.* New ed. Rosheim: Maisonneuve, 1984.

Sebillot, Paul. *Le Folklore de la France.* New ed. 8 volumes. Paris: P.U.F., 1982–1986.

Siculus, Diodorus. *Library of History.* 12 volumes. Boston: Harvard/Loeb Classical Library, 1933.

Sjoestedt, M. L., trans. *Revue celtique,* vol. 43.

Stokes, Whitley. *Three Irish Glossaries.* London: Williams and Norgate, 1862.

Strabo. *Geography.* 8 volumes. Boston: Harvard/Loeb Classical Library, 1917.

Thomas, Dylan. *Deaths and Entrances.* London: Dent and Sons, 1957.

Toutain, Jules. *Les Cultes païens dans l'Empire romain.* Volume 3. Paris: Ernest Leroux, 1921.

Van Gennep, Arnold. *Manuel de Folklore contemporain.* Paris: Stock, 1935–1958.

Index